AMTRAK'S HISTORY

Through Its Equipment

BRIAN SOLOMON

Dedication

To the late William Garrison, a lifelong railroader who encouraged my railroad interest from an early age.

Acknowledgments

There isn't space to properly credit everyone that helped me over the last 50 years during my travels, research and photography involved with this book. My father's vast collection of photographs and railroad literature helped establish a foundation from which I built a much larger library and overall understanding of passenger trains and the machines behind them. Among the collection's gems are many original documents from the era of the High-Speed Ground Transportation Act as well as public brochures, timetables, and other literature from a bygone era. In addition to bringing me on many of my early train rides — including an unforgettable journey on the United Aircraft TurboTrain — my father also assisted with editing this text.

Invaluable to this project are my many friends and colleagues in the railroad industry who facilitated my travels and understanding of operations and equipment. Thanks to their generosity, I've visited dispatching centers, signal towers, and locomotive shops, as well as the inner sanctums at major stations and terminals. I've traveled on locomotives and experienced theatre/inspection car *American View*, among many other opportunities beyond the reach of the average paying passenger. My research took me beyond our borders — I've spent more than 25 years exploring railroads across Europe and Japan. I've traveled on Britain's HST, Germany's ICE, France's TGV, among others.

The members of the Irish Railway Record Society gave me unrestricted access to their vast archives and facilitated intellectual discussion on many aspects of railroad technologies and operations, including a detailed understanding of the operation of EMD diesel-electric locomotives. Among the domestic archives that contributed to my research are: the UMass Library in Amherst, Mass., University of Wisconsin's Wendt Library, David P. Morgan Library at Firecrown, Railroad Museum of Pennsylvania's archives, Pennsylvania State Archives in Harrisburg, and San Francisco Public Library. In the mid-1990s, I worked as an associate editor of *Passenger Train Journal* and editor of *Pacific RailNews*, which opened countless doors and gave me an operating knowledge of railroad journalism.

Special thanks for help with photography: Mike Abalos, Marshall Beecher, Kurt Bell, Scott Bontz, Robert A. Buck, Dave Clinton, Dan Cupper, Mike Danneman, Tom Danneman, Tim Doherty, Doug Eisele, Chris Guss, Mike Gardner, Paul Goewey, Dick Gruber, John Gruber, Scott A. Hartley, David Hegarty, Mark Hemphill, T.S. Hoover, Dan Howard, Brian Jennison, Clark Johnson, Jr., Bob Karambeles, Tom Kline, George W. Kowanski, Mark Leppert, Fred Matthews, Jack May, Doug Moore, Denis McCabe, Joe McMillan, Scott Muskopf, Claire Nolan, John Peters, John Pickett, Rich Reed, Pete Reusch, Doug Riddell, Jon Roma, Paul Roth, Brian Rutherford, J.D. Schmid, Brian Schmidt, Jeffrey T. Schultz, Carl Swanson, J. Craig Thorpe, Otto M. Vondrak, Patrick Yough, and Walter E. Zullig, Jr.

Thanks to my brother Sean and my mother, Maureen, for accompanying me on many Amtrak trips, and my wife, Kris, for her support as a travel companion, her photography and editing, as well as helping me seek out places to watch and travel on Amtrak.

Special thanks to my editor, Jeff Wilson, and to Kelly Katlaps and the design staff at Firecrown Media for transforming words, photos, and ideas into this book. During my research, many people have assisted me with tracking down information, and I've consulted hundreds of sources — most of which are listed in the bibliography. I've done my best in the time allotted to present accurate information. However, owing to the relative complexity of the subject and the vast amount of information that I needed to distill, while sometimes facing contradictory descriptions and discrepancies in source materials, it is possible that errors may have crept into this work. If so, these errors are my own. — *Brian Solomon*

On the cover: Amtrak's *California Zephyr* departs Chicago Union Station behind Genesis P40 diesels on August 28, 1994. *Brian Solomon*

Back cover: Amtrak silver GG1 No. 906 pauses on its way to Washington, D.C., for display on April 21, 1977. Trailing it are an E60CP, plus both the borrowed European locomotives: ASEA Rc4 X995 and French built-Alstom electric X996. *Amtrak; Ed Wojtas*

Firecrown Media Inc.,
405 Cherry Street
Chattanooga, TN 37402
Shop.Trains.com

Published in 2025
29 28 27 26 25   1 2 3 4 5

Manufactured in China

ISBN: 979-8-89491-019-2
EISBN: 979-8-89491-020-8

Editor: Jeff Wilson
Book Design: Kelly Katlaps

CONTENTS

TOP: To many, the most attractive livery applied to Amtrak's Metroliner cars was this variation of the Phase I scheme: broad vertical red, white, and blue striping, adapted to the shapes of the panels on the leading car ends. This scheme was introduced in 1972 but the fleet was not uniformly treated. *Paul Roth*

BOTTOM: Amtrak AEM7 electric No. 940 leads a northbound Northeast Direct train across the Susquehanna River at Perryville, Md., in November 1997. *Brian Solomon*

INTRODUCTION

Since childhood, I have embraced the thrill of Amtrak travel and relish train journeys near and far. I have made countless journeys on trains from Maine to Southern California. I am just old enough to remember long-distance travel before Amtrak. As a child I traveled with my parents on Burlington Northern's *North Coast Limited* from Seattle across Montana, made overnight journeys on Seaboard Coast Line to Florida, and took trips over the former New Haven on Penn Central.

Among my earliest memories was going to New York's Penn Station with my mother to meet my father off a train — and not just any train, but the special inaugural run of the new *Metroliner*. This sticks in my mind because moments after my father put me on his shoulders, he exclaimed that his camera had been

stolen (along with his photos from the day). We may have lost those pictures, but we still have the invitational packet given to journalists, and the memory of later *Metroliner* experiences has stayed with me for more than a half century.

The *Metroliner* was more than just a train, and its 50-plus-year story offers an encapsulation of Amtrak, which also helps tie the story of its equipment together. As I write this in 2024, some Metroliner cars survive in daily service as control coach cab-cars, which I see pass on the *Keystone* trains that run almost hourly through Lancaster, Pa., near where my wife and I now live.

I hope to convey my enthusiasm for Amtrak through the illustrations of its equipment. Many are photos that I exposed, and they represent my efforts over more than 40 years to document the technology and history of Amtrak's trains and operations. The text surveys more than a half century of Amtrak locomotives and rolling stock to tell a story of the development of American passenger trains. This offers insight into the design and intended applications, as well as the specifications, service, and comparative success of various equipment used by Amtrak. I hope to provide a contextual understanding to help explain the great variety of equipment used by Amtrak and why some equipment has worked in daily service for more than five decades, while other equipment, despite great promise, saw only brief service.

Where practical, I discuss equipment in detail, not to focus on minutia but rather to use detail to highlight advances in technological development

Mel Patrick exposed this atmospheric view of Train 52, the snow-covered Miami/St. Petersburg-bound *Floridian* bathed in steam at Chicago Union Station on a frigid February day in 1972. A carryover from the steam era, Amtrak operated traditional steam-heated passenger cars during its first decade of operations. Steam heat ended in 1981, but it outlasted the *Floridian,* which was among the trains discontinued in 1979. *Mel Patrick*

Racing out of the setting sun on January 16, 2015, new Siemens ACS64 No. 623 whisks Thursday- and Friday-only Northeast Regional Train 134 at Marcus Hook, Pa. The ACS64, also known as a Cities Sprinter, is a thoroughly modern locomotive and the backbone of Amtrak's electric locomotive fleet, providing high-speed service along the busy Northeast Corridor. *Brian Solomon*

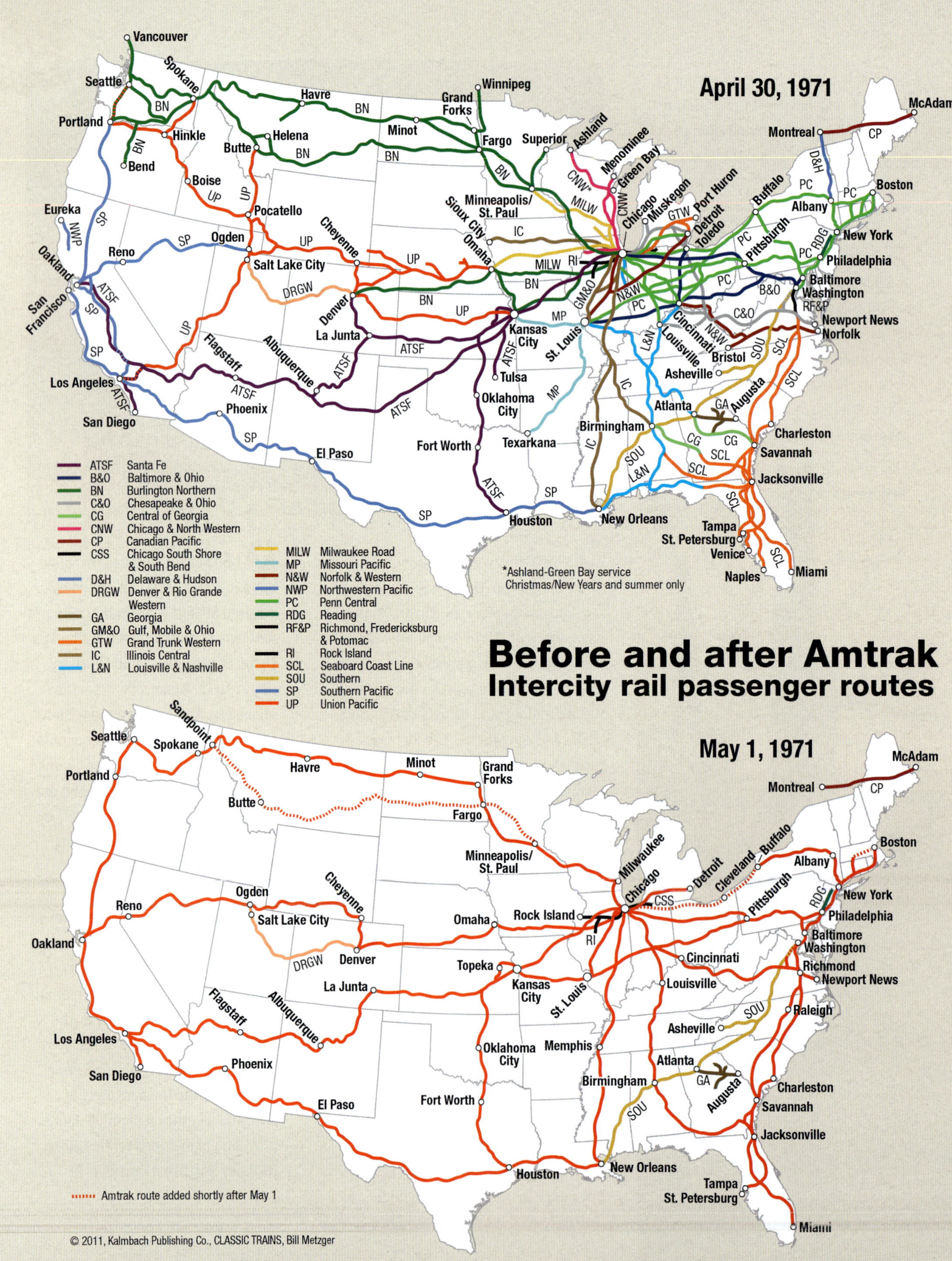
Before and after Amtrak
Intercity rail passenger routes
April 30, 1971
ATSF Santa Fe
B&O Baltimore & Ohio
BN Burlington Northern
C&O Chesapeake & Ohio
CG Central of Georgia
CNW Chicago & North Western
CP Canadian Pacific
CSS Chicago South Shore & South Bend
D&H Delaware & Hudson
DRGW Denver & Rio Grande Western
GA Georgia
GM&O Gulf, Mobile & Ohio
GTW Grand Trunk Western
IC Illinois Central
L&N Louisville & Nashville
MILW Milwaukee Road
MP Missouri Pacific
N&W Norfolk & Western
NWP Northwestern Pacific
PC Penn Central
RDG Reading
RF&P Richmond, Fredericksburg & Potomac
RI Rock Island
SCL Seaboard Coast Line
SOU Southern
SP Southern Pacific
UP Union Pacific
*Ashland-Green Bay service Christmas/New Years and summer only
Vancouver
Seattle
Spokane
Portland
Hinkle
Bend
Boise
Havre
Helena
Butte
Pocatello
Winnipeg
Grand Forks
Minot
Fargo
Superior
Ashland
Menominee
Green Bay
Minneapolis/ St. Paul
Sioux City
Omaha
Chicago
Muskegon
Port Huron
Detroit
Toledo
Eureka
Reno
Ogden
Salt Lake City
Cheyenne
Denver
Oakland
San Francisco
La Junta
Kansas City
St. Louis
Flagstaff
Albuquerque
Tulsa
Oklahoma City
Los Angeles
San Diego
Phoenix
El Paso
Fort Worth
Texarkana
Houston
New Orleans
Birmingham
Atlanta
Augusta
Asheville
Bristol
Louisville
Cincinnati
Pittsburgh
Buffalo
Albany
Montreal
McAdam
Boston
New York
Philadelphia
Baltimore
Washington
Newport News
Norfolk
Charleston
Savannah
Jacksonville
Tampa
St. Petersburg
Venice
Naples
Miami
May 1, 1971
Sandpoint
Milwaukee
Rock Island
Topeka
Cleveland
Memphis
Richmond
Raleigh
Amtrak route added shortly after May 1
© 2011, Kalmbach Publishing Co., CLASSIC TRAINS, Bill Metzger

and to help distinguish various types of equipment from one another. Often the outward appearance of locomotives and rolling stock may only hint at the defining components and systems that are most important. While some details are little more than superficial trappings, others delineate crucial differences that may directly relate to performance, application, reliability, and longevity.

For example, when we observe the three varieties of GE's Genesis locomotives they appear outwardly similar, but within their bodies lurk important technological differences. The discussion of these differences is crucial to understanding the real-life applications for these locomotives — such as why the P42DCs are used all around the country and why the 700-series P32AC-DMs work Empire Service trains to New York City.

I describe Amtrak's myriad paint schemes and how these have been applied over the years. By and large, I discuss the details of Amtrak's liveries using the context of its own standard groupings as prescribed in its *Railroad Livery and Logo Guide.* For many observers this is a comparatively recent delineation of the variations of paint worn by Amtrak equipment over a half century. Amtrak describes its liveries as "phases," which tends to group similar schemes from the periods of time when they were in vogue. Confusing matters is the considerable overlap between some phases and the impossibly short spans for others.

To help demonstrate Amtrak diversity, I've included many different types of equipment, with illustrations covering different periods as well as changes through rebuilding or other functional adaptions. I've offered geographical variety by including photographs of many different trains, while including many services that have been discontinued or rebranded over the years.

← These maps show American long-distance passenger routes before and after Amtrak's start date on May 1, 1971. You can easily see the extent to which passenger service was cut at startup. Commuter rail routes are largely omitted. *Trains Magazine*

↓ Amtrak's fifth annual National Train Day in Chicago was a few hours away as the Heritage trainset lead by NPCU No. 406 (an F40PH rebuilt to a control/baggage car) and P42 156 await positioning at Union Station. The equipment was used to provide three 40-minute public train rides around Amtrak's Chicago-area trackage on May 11, 2012. *Chris Guss*

On March 21, 2023, new Siemens Charger (ALC42) No. 304 leads the Portland section of the *Empire Builder,* Train 27, westward on BNSF near Stevenson, Wash. Passengers are treated to mile after mile of stunning scenery along the broad Columbia River. Amtrak continues to invest in new equipment for trains across its system. *Chris Guss*

Compare these photos from Birmingham, Ala., from 1979 and 2018. The top view was made on April 9, 1979, shortly after Amtrak assumed operation of the Southern Railway's *Crescent,* pictured alongside Amtrak Train 56, the *Floridian*. At bottom, Genesis P42 No. 124 leads Train 19, the New Orleans-bound *Crescent*, on December 16, 2018. Today in many parts of America, only a lone daily Amtrak train serves stations that were built in an earlier era for a much greater level of business. *Top: J. David Ingles; Bottom: Brian Solomon*

However, while I've scoured dozens of collections and perused thousands of photographs, it is not my intention to provide a comprehensive catalog of Amtrak's rolling stock. Furthermore, by virtue of its creation, operation, and partnerships, not all Amtrak service has employed equipment owned, painted, or lettered for Amtrak. In some cases, I've delved into the peculiarities of financing, leasing, or ownership; in others I have not. Among the hallmarks of diversity across the network has been Amtrak's operation of state-sponsored services. In this discussion, I aim to achieve an appreciation for the effects of these relationships in terms of train operations and equipment choices rather than delving into the details, complexities, politics, and evolution of the relationships themselves.

One of the common threads in this book is how Amtrak needed to adapt equipment to its needs. In its earliest days, Amtrak had little choice but to work with locomotives and cars built for its operational antecedents — the private common-carrier railroads — which for more than 140 years had provided American intercity passenger services. In some instances, inherited equipment was designed for specific applications that continued under Amtrak (such as the *Metroliner*), but often Amtrak had to make do with equipment nearing the end of its expected service life that was intended for circumstances and services quite different than what Amtrak needed. In other words, Amtrak made due with what it had.

Early in its existence, Amtrak began looking to buy new locomotives and cars that were better suited to what various services required. This was complicated by the lack of a domestic industry focused on products of the modern long-distance passenger train. By 1970, domestic locomotive manufacturers were focused on building heavy freight locomotives. Passenger car suppliers had largely subsisted on construction of rapid transit vehicles and, to a lesser extent, commuter cars. Owing to the lack of investment in long-distance trains since the 1950s, and the precipitous decline of the passenger train business, the industry struggled to supply modern railcars on short notice.

As a result, Amtrak made the bold and necessary move to explore adapting trains from overseas. This began in 1972

with the import of ANF Turbotrains from France, and has continued throughout Amtrak's tenure up to the present by adapting European train designs in the form of locomotives and passenger cars from Siemens Mobility and high-speed trainsets built by Alstom that blend Italian tilting technology with modern high-speed French propulsion systems.

Yet, arguably, some of the most enduring equipment in Amtrak's fleet were products of American ingenuity, notably the Amfleet cars built by Budd in the 1970s, the Superliner engineered by Pullman-Standard, and diesel-electric locomotives built by EMD and General Electric. By this book's publication in 2025, the oldest Amfleet cars will have seen nearly 50 years of service and the oldest of GE's Genesis diesels (the P40s of 1993) will have more service years behind them than did most of the functional E and F antiques inherited by Amtrak at its startup in 1971.

Among the challenges facing Amtrak and its suppliers is designing and building trains that make the best use of the latest technology and still maintaining compatibility and interoperability with existing equipment without major modification to infrastructure, all while ensuring durability to withstand the brutal effects of years of daily operation. The equipment that has survived the longest is a testimony to the men and women that designed, built, maintain, and operate it.

A five-unit TurboTrain led by power car 51 waits to depart Boston's South Station in the early 1970s. The contrast of the sleek, modern train in the badly decayed terminal was indicative of the state of passenger railroading in the period. United Aircraft's TurboTrain had offered a quick way to provide faster train service without expensive infrastructure improvement. *Paul Roth*

CHAPTER 1

Early self-pro

Rail Diesel Cars, Metroliners, and turbo trains played key roles in Amtrak's early development

In September 1989, a Rohr Industries-built RTL Turboliner races along New York's Hudson River past Bannerman Castle north of Breakneck Ridge on its way from Albany-Rensselaer to Grand Central Terminal. Bought new by Amtrak, the gas-turbine-powered trains had a distinctly styled cab/power car at each end. The Turboliners played important roles in several corridors in Amtrak's early years of operations. *Brian Solomon*

Self-propelled trains have played integral roles in Amtrak service since its creation in 1971. While the number of self-propelled rail vehicles is relatively small in comparison with Amtrak's total fleet of locomotives and passenger cars, these trains are significant because of the large numbers of riders they have carried, their high visibility to the general public, and their effects on further development of rail equipment and rail services. Although their operations have been restricted to specific regional services, millions of travelers have experienced Amtrak's Metroliner cars, Empire Service Turboliners, and Acela Express HSTs.

On Labor Day 1975, Amtrak's eastbound *Blackhawk* (Dubuque, Iowa-Chicago) consisted of three RDCs as it passed the boarded-up Illinois Central Gulf depot at Genoa, Ill. Weekdays the eastward train ran as No. 370, while on Sundays and select holidays it had a later schedule as No. 372. The *Blackhawk* was discontinued in 1981; the structure, however, remained standing in 2024. *David Franzen*

Amtrak's self-propelled trains largely fall into two categories: multiple unit (MU) cars, where each vehicle has its own propulsion system but is designed to work in tandem with similar vehicles — such as the Budd-built Rail Diesel Cars (RDCs) and overhead-electric Metroliner cars — and non-standard, semipermanently coupled trainsets propelled by purpose-built power cars, such as high-speed electric train sets designed for

Acela Express service and the various types of turbo-powered trains.

The Canadian-designed and -built LRC trains that were experimentally operated by Amtrak in Northeast Corridor service between 1980 and 1982 do not strictly meet these criteria for self-propelled trains. However, I'm including them here because the LRC's specially designed cars and locomotives were built to work together, and these trains contributed to the further testing, development, and application of advanced trainsets that used self-propelled arrangements. Not included in this section are Amtrak's Talgo trains, which — although they have used highly specialized train sets — were built to be powered by conventional diesel-electric locomotives.

Elsewhere in the world, purpose-built self-propelled trains have enjoyed widespread application in long-distance and local passenger services. In many countries, these trains have largely replaced traditional locomotive-powered flexible consists. Self-propelled trains offer a variety of advantages. They allow for practical application of advanced railcar designs that take advantage of specialized equipment or systems that may not be easily made

An early version of Amtrak's Arrow logo covers the Penn Central noodle on the uniquely styled Budd RDCs built for New Haven's five-car *Roger Williams* in 1955. Seen shortly after Amtrak's startup, this once-famous trainset idled amongst the litter, decaying canopies, and oil-saturated, misaligned trackage at Boston's South Station — which had once been the busiest station in the United States. *Paul Roth*

Amtrak eventually repainted the *Roger Williams* RDCs with red noses, but the old Arrow logo remained the same. Amtrak numbered the cars 27 and 28.
George W. Kowanski

compatible with traditional equipment. Self-propelled trains are preferred for high-speed services, where rapid acceleration, light axle weight, and route-specific clearances are necessary or desirable. The disadvantages of many self-propelled trains have included functionally inflexible consists, operational incompatibility with other equipment, and specialized maintenance requirements.

Budd RDCs: Nos. 10-43

North American railroads were early to adopt mass-produced diesel multiple-unit cars, in the form of Budd's Rail Diesel Car. These were variously configured for commuter, regional, and long-distance passenger travel. The Budd RDC enjoyed moderate success in the 1950s, and a few railroads made good use of these versatile cars to lower operating costs and improve their passenger

This trailing view shows a lone Connecticut Department of Transportation (CDOT) SPV-2000 working as Train 470 at Windsor Locks, Conn., on July 7, 1983. It's bound for Springfield, Mass., on the former New Haven. *Brian Solomon*

service. However, Amtrak only inherited a small number of RDCs, and these only played minor roles in its national operations. In the 1980s and 1990s Amtrak revisited diesel multiple units, but found that these types of cars did not offer desirable solutions despite great success on railroads in Europe and elsewhere around the world.

In 1949, the Budd Company debuted the RDC — a brilliant re-adaptation of an old idea. From the early years of the 20th century, a variety of manufacturers led by Electro-Motive Corp. (EMC) had supplied American railroads with self-propelled cars powered with internal-combustion (gas or distillate) engines. These worked with varying success in light passenger service. In developing its RDC, Budd pushed the self-propelled internal combustion powered railcar to a new level. Like Budd's other passenger cars, the RDC benefitted from the company's patented shot-welded stainless-steel construction. This featured elegant side fluting, which gave the body great strength with relatively light weight. The cars incorporated a variety of innovative features and superior design characteristics that overcame many limitations that faced earlier railcars. The RDC was remarkably versatile, reliable, safe, and comfortable.

In contrast to the old "doodlebugs," Budd's RDC was a double-ended car with a full set of operator's controls, headlights, and horns at each end. This greatly simplified changing directions at terminals (especially on branch lines) and allowed railroads great flexibility in assignments, as they required no specialized facilities or turntables.

Integral to the RDC's design was its propulsion system, which adapted a compact, high-output two-cycle diesel engine developed during World War II for use in tanks. Pairs of these 275-hp engines, built by General Motors subsidiary Detroit Diesel, were mounted below the body of the car. Power was transmitted to the drive wheels using a torque-converter transmission. Roof-mounted radiator intake vents brought in cooling air for the engine and gave the car its characteristic hump-backed appearance. Unlike earlier internal-combustion railcars that operated singly or occasionally hauled an unpowered trailer, the RDC was designed for multiple-unit operation with any number of cars electrically connected to work together under one common throttle.

The RDC was built in several configurations that allowed railroads to assign the cars to a great variety of short- and long-distance services. The model RDC-1 was the most common type, with its full interior compartment devoted to passenger seating. Other variations included the RDC-2, which divided the compartment between a seating area and a baggage compartment; the RDC-3, with baggage and Railway Post Office (RPO) sections in addition to seats; the RDC-4, which was exclusively a baggage car/RPO unit, and the RDC-9, a specialized cabless type intended as center car working in multiple with other RDCs.

The RDC lowered operating costs, and a key goal of their use was saving

Budd RDC-2 No. 35 rests between runs on a sunny November 1975 afternoon at New Haven, Conn. In its first 15 years, Amtrak routinely assigned Budd RDCs to the Springfield, Mass.-New Haven shuttle trains that connected with through Boston-New York runs.
George W. Kowanski

money on lightly traveled routes and suburban lines. New York Central was the first to buy RDCs, having trialed a demonstration car in 1950. Initially assigned to the Boston & Albany, they were advertised as *Beeliners* and worked in both mainline and branch-line services. Other New England railroads took notice, with Boston & Maine and New Haven rapidly emerging as the most intensive RDC operators. Although largely concentrated in the East, several Western lines had notable RDC runs. Longest was Western Pacific, which assigned its pair of RDC-2s to service as *Zephyrettes* on the 924-mile run between Salt Lake City, Utah and Oakland, Calif.

Amtrak inherited 24 RDCs, numbered from 10 to 43, from a variety of original owners. The largest group came from Penn Central, including a pair of specially styled former New Haven cars with fiberglass locomotive-nose front ends that were built in 1956 for the Boston-New York *Roger Williams* streamliner. From Burlington Northern it acquired cars that originally worked for Great Northern and Northern Pacific, as well as the two WP cars.

The majority of Amtrak's RDCs worked New England routes. Cars were based at New Haven for service on the New Haven-Hartford-Springfield shuttle, typically singly or in pairs. A few cars remained in this service into the 1980s. In the mid-1970s, several RDCs were briefly assigned to the *Blackhawk* over the Illinois Central Gulf between Chicago and Dubuque, Iowa.

After their Amtrak service, some RDCs were sold. Number 18 worked for a several owners and was ultimately acquired by New Hampshire's Conway Scenic Railroad, which restored it to its original New Haven No. 23 and named it *Millie.* Working as a single car, it is used for special events and extra trains.

In January 1986, a Connecticut DOT Budd SPV-2000 idles between runs at Springfield, Mass. The CDOT purchased 13 SPVs, assigning most to the Amtrak-operated New Haven-Springfield shuttles. Others worked commuter branch lines. *Brian Solomon*

"Amtrak inherited 24 RDCs, numbered 10 to 43, from a variety of original owners. The largest group came from Penn Central."

SPV-2000: 988-999

The success of Budd's original RDC and the perceived demand for an energy-efficient, versatile self-propelled train led the company to reinvent its car. In 1977, it introduced a modern self-propelled Metroliner derivative that appeared to overcome some of the shortcomings of the original cars. Budd's model SPV-2000 (Self-Propelled Vehicle, expected to work to the year 2000) employed the curved-sided Metro-shell body that had been successfully mass produced for Amfleet passenger cars. The SPV was heavier and significantly more powerful than the original RDC, using a pair of 360-hp Detroit Diesel engines. All four axles are powered, instead of just two as on the RDC.

The prototype was a sharp-looking car with modern styling that set it apart from many of the rolling antiques operating in Eastern passenger service. After a tour of regional commuter rail systems, the Connecticut Department of Transportation ordered 13 cars for delivery in mid-1980 for branch operations on intrastate lines and on the Amtrak-operated New Haven-Hartford-Springfield shuttles. These had seats for 85 passengers in the standard two-by-two row configuration. All of

the cars were painted in the Phase III livery, similar to Amfleet I. A dozen cars were numbered 988-999 and carried both Amtrak and CDOT logos, while a lone car, No. 50, came in Amtrak livery but with only CDOT markings. The cars were clean and bright inside and offered a smooth ride, but despite Budd's design efforts, overall interest in the SPV-2000 proved marginal. Including its overseas sales, Budd only built 30 cars. They unfortunately suffered from low reliability, which on occasion led to Amtrak towing failed SPV's with its antique Alco RS3s or other diesels to maintain schedules. In 1986, Amtrak replaced the SPVs on the Springfield run with F40PH diesels leading one- and two-car trains. A decade later Amtrak imported Danish IC3 diesel railcars for demonstration services (see page 58).

Metroliner: 800 series

In many respects the Metroliner story is the beginning chapter of the Amtrak story itself, and the history of the Metroliner cars have been woven through the first five and a half decades of Amtrak's active fleet. Although the Metroliner cars and the high-speed *Metroliner* service for which they were

↑ A CDOT SPV, No. 998, brings up the rear of Train No. 190 eastbound on the former New Haven at Mamaroneck, N.Y., on June 28, 1981. One of the intended advantages of Budd's SPV-2000 was that it could operate in-consist at the back of an Amfleet train, which would allow Springfield-New Haven shuttles to couple onto through Northeast Corridor trains, eliminating the need for passengers to change trains at New Haven. It sounded good in theory, but in practice it was tried only briefly. *Walter E. Zullig, Jr.*

Train 121, a Washington D.C-bound *Metroliner,* races through Edison, N.J., at 4:55 p.m. on April 10, 1977. The original Budd Metroliner cars served in *Metroliner* service until 1981. In the lead is snack-bar coach No. 858. Below the number you can still see a shadow of the Pennsylvania Railroad keystone logo that originally adorned the car. *George W. Kowanski*

858

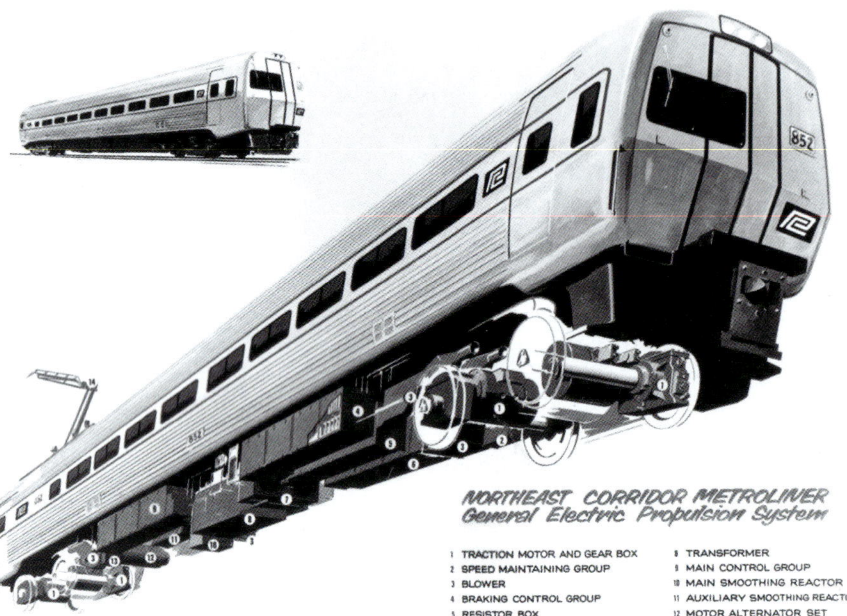

General Electric and Westinghouse independently supplied propulsion for various Metroliner cars. This illustration depicts key features of GE's system, including traction motors, gear units, solid state control, and static battery charging equipment that was applied to snack bar-coaches and Metro Club cars. Westinghouse supplied equipment for Metroliner coaches. *General Electric; collection of Richard Jay Solomon*

designed appeared inseparable during the early years, today it's important to distinguish the equipment from the service because the original Metroliner cars only worked in *Metroliner* service until 1981, but have continued to serve Amtrak.

Japan's Shinkansen made its debut in 1964, coinciding with the Tokyo World's Fair. This stunning modern railroad sparked great interest in the potential of high-speed trains at a time when privately operated passenger trains in the United States had been suffering precipitous declines. The Shinkansen was an all-new purpose-built 320-mile railroad running from the center of Tokyo to Osaka with 10 intermediate stops serving some of the nation's densest population centers. Key to its success was dramatically shortening travel times while offering high capacity and frequent departures — up to 30 round trips a day. What mesmorized America about the "Bullet Train" (as it was popularly known in the United States), was its maximum speed of 130

mph. This cut running time between Tokyo and Osaka to just 4 hours from the more than 6 hours required by the traditional railroad. In less than 20 years, Japan had emerged from the ashes of World War II to running the fastest daily trains in the world.

America's busiest travel corridor is in the Northeast from New York through Philadelphia to Washington, D.C. In the 1930s, with federal assistance, the Pennsylvania Railroad electrified its lines connecting these cities. While this remained America's foremost intercity passenger route, by the

Metroliner coach 820 displays Amtrak Phase I paint as it glides by several stored Southern Railway E8As at Ivy City in Washington D.C., in the early 1980s. This car was later rebuilt as control coach 9648 for push-pull service. *Paul Roth*

early 1960s it faced declining ridership stemming from increased competition from airlines and highways. In 1961, Eastern Airlines introduced hourly shuttle service between New York and Washington that rapidly captured premium business travelers. In 1963, Interstate 95 was completed between the cities, allowing faster travel times for motorists, especially among intermediate points.

Despite these transportation improvements, the continued growth of the region and ever greater needs for passenger capacity, combined with deterioration of rail service, led Senator Claiborne Pell of Rhode Island to seek a long-term solution. He sought to guide and fund improvements to railroad passenger service across the Northeast and pushed for passage of the High-Speed Ground Transportation Act, which was supported by President Lyndon Johnson and passed into law in September 1965. This established federal funding for improvements to passenger service between Washington, New York, and Boston.

At the time, PRR and New York Central were involved in complex merger negotiations that led to the Penn Central in 1968 (and PC was also compelled to absorb the struggling New Haven Railroad in 1969). The conditions leading up to Penn Central encouraged the railroads to cooperate with public passenger-service initiatives. The PRR in particular recognized that working with the federal government aided its merger effort.

Early on, two high-profile projects emerged: the electric-powered Metroliner, intended to speed service between Washington and New York; and TurboTrain, developed to speed service on the New Haven between New York and Boston (see page 34).

The Pennsylvania, working with consulting engineers Louis T. Klauder and Associates in cooperation with the Department of Commerce's Northeast Corridor Transportation Project, drafted detailed specifications for creation of advanced exceptionally high-speed electric multiple-unit trains for a proposed "High Speed Demonstration Project between New York and Washington." The railroad had been developing mainline self-propelled electrically powered multiple-unit cars since the early 1900s and operated one of the most extensive fleets of these cars in the United States. However, where in America MUs had been viewed ideal for suburban services, it really wasn't until the advent of the Shink-

Soon after Amtrak's startup, a New York City-bound *Metroliner* passes the Ivy City terminal a few minutes after departing Washington Union Station. In the lead is Metro Club Car 883, which displays hastily applied Amtrak patches on the front and sides. *Paul Roth*

ansen's Bullet Trains that a U.S. railroad considered the potential of MUs as a high-speed long-distance train.

This was a significant change in the way an American railroad viewed long-distance passenger trains. In its 155-page specifications document, PRR detailed a thoroughly modern train. It expanded on the design that PRR and the Budd Company had collaborated on since the late 1950s to create a modern fleet of suburban trains (based on Budd's experimental Pioneer III lightweight coach; later known as Silverliners). It specified that the "carbody shall be constructed of stainless steel assembled by resistance welding, unless otherwise specified," and that "all primary

↑ The Washington-New York City *Metroliner* was at the forefront of Amtrak's early advertising, focusing on the heavily traveled Northeast Corridor. This ad was included in Amtrak's June 11, 1972 public timetable. *Amtrak; collection of Richard Jay Solomon*

A four-unit Metroliner set shows off recently rebuilt cars in fresh paint as it flies through Princeton Junction, N.J., on July 6, 1980. *Howard Paulma*

Metroliner's on-board phones were a state-of-the-art novelty in 1969 when Penn Central advertised the coin-operated pay phones as the "fastest phone in the East" — an ironic allusion to the gunslingers of the old West as popularized by Hollywood. *Penn Central; collection of Richard Jay Solomon*

structural members in the car framing shall be constructed of austenitic stainless steel (which contains an established percentage of nickel in its composition)." This described the basic patented welded stainless-steel construction that defined Budd passenger car designs since its revolutionary streamlined trains of the 1930s. Although bids were solicited from other American car manufactures (including Pullman-Standard), Budd was clearly PRR's preferred builder. The details, such as the specifications for the side sheets, spelled out this preference: "Stainless steel sheets having longitudinal corrugations or flutes spaced 1" to 4" apart, shall be welded to the outside of the posts in the space below the windows and between the side doors."

The specification included great detail on appearance and passenger accommodations as well as its propulsion and other key elements of its design. The train's front (A-end) was described: "The general appearance shall be a modified rounded end with slight sloping to give a pleasing appearance."

The contract to construct 50 Metroliner cars was awarded in 1966, and this was later expanded to 61 units. Contracts for electrical propulsion were divided between General Electric and Westinghouse. In addition, there were four Metroliner test cars (numbered T-1 to T-4) built in December 1966 for the Department of Commerce that were based on Budd's earlier Silverliner design.

The 61 production cars were built to the following specifications: the length was 85 feet over coupler faces, trucks were the GS1 equalized type with outboard journals with 36" wheels and an 8'-6" wheelbase, and truck spacing was 59'-6" between centers. Cars were built with three distinct seating configurations. Using PRR's classification system, these were: class MP85E4 (Nos. 800-830), 76-seat coaches built with Westinghouse electricals; class MPC85E4 (850-869), 60-seat snack-bar coaches; and MPP85E5, 35-seat Metro Club cars. Both of the latter types had GE electrical gear. All, regardless of configuration, had the distinctive cab and controls at the A-end. The first cars were completed in November 1967.

Metroliner had been promoted as a 160-mph train, and in late 1967 some of the cars reached 164 mph on a test run that fulfilled the letter of the design. For a variety of reasons, the trains never approached anywhere near the top design speed in revenue service. The Metroliner's sleek appearance and sophisticated innovative design offered a vision of the future, but unfortunately was beset with myriad electrical and mechanical problems that delayed the beginning of regular service and ultimately limited their practical applications and continued to plague the trainsets for years to come.

Metroliner to Amtrak

The Metroliner cars were delivered with PRR keystones on the cab ends, but *Metroliner* service didn't make its debut until January 16, 1969, almost a year after consummation of Penn Central. Metroliner proved an instant success with train riders who benefited from its fast schedules and were delighted by its modern comforts. Among the distinctive features was a coin-operated touch-tone train phone. In the days before cell phones, a train phone was a delightful transportation novelty.

However, the trains' technical problems continued, but these were relatively small issues compared with the

On May 31, 2024, Amtrak control coach 9633 leads *Keystone* No. 651 at Leaman Place (Paradise), Pa. This was originally Metroliner coach 830, rebuilt in October 1987 as a control coach for push-pull service with Amfleet equipment. In 2024, the surviving former Metroliner control coaches represent a continuous thread that weaves together the Amtrak story. *Brian Solomon*

Top: On May 15, 1971, just two weeks after Amtrak assumed operation of American intercity passenger services, UA TurboTrain 50 departs the Syracuse, N.Y., station at the west end of Penn Central's former New York Central DeWitt Yard.
Frank M. Klock

Bottom: The United Aircraft TurboTrain was originally configured in a three-unit articulated set with dome power cars at both ends. Capable of 171 mph, these aerodynamic trains represented a vision of the future in the early days of Amtrak.
U.S. DOT; courtesy of Dan Cupper

growing financial maelstrom surrounding Penn Central itself.

Instead of the merger serving as the hoped-for panacea to the two railroads' financial problems, it worsened the issues. As PC rapidly deteriorated, the federal government recognized the necessity of providing meaningful relief for its money-losing, long-distance passenger business. Government involvement that began with the High-Speed Ground Transportation Act soon took on a much larger implications.

On January 18, 1970, the U.S. Department of Transportation announced its plan to support a national passenger rail network, which went beyond the need to simply solve PC's problems, aiming to address the broad national situation. The solution needed to avoid the appearance of federally operated passenger trains, which was viewed as politically untenable. Instead, a government-created passenger rail organization called Railpax was patterned on the quasi-public corporation that operated communications satellites.

Events progressed more rapidly than anyone expected. In March, Penn Central petitioned to discontinue all passenger service west of Harrisburg, Pa., and Buffalo, N.Y. In response, Railpax legislation was introduced in the U.S. Senate in May 1970 and passed in June. That month, PC declared bankruptcy — it was the largest U.S. corporate failure to that time. In October, Congress passed the Rail Passenger Service Act, which was signed into law by President Richard M. Nixon at the end of the month. Among the purposes of the Act were "to provide financial assistance for and establishment of a national rail passenger system, to provide for the modernization of railroad passenger equipment, to authorize the prescribing of minimum standards for railroad passenger service."

It took months to hash out the details. On May 1, 1971, with little more than a tiny budget, a new name, and a logo, Amtrak assumed responsibility not just for *Metroliner* operations, but for all of PC's remaining long-distance services as well as those of 16 other railroads. A caveat to this change was that approximately half of the long-haul passenger trains in the United States were discontinued on the eve of Amtrak, leaving the new company with 184 daily intercity trains — the majority of which operated on Northeastern Penn Central routes.

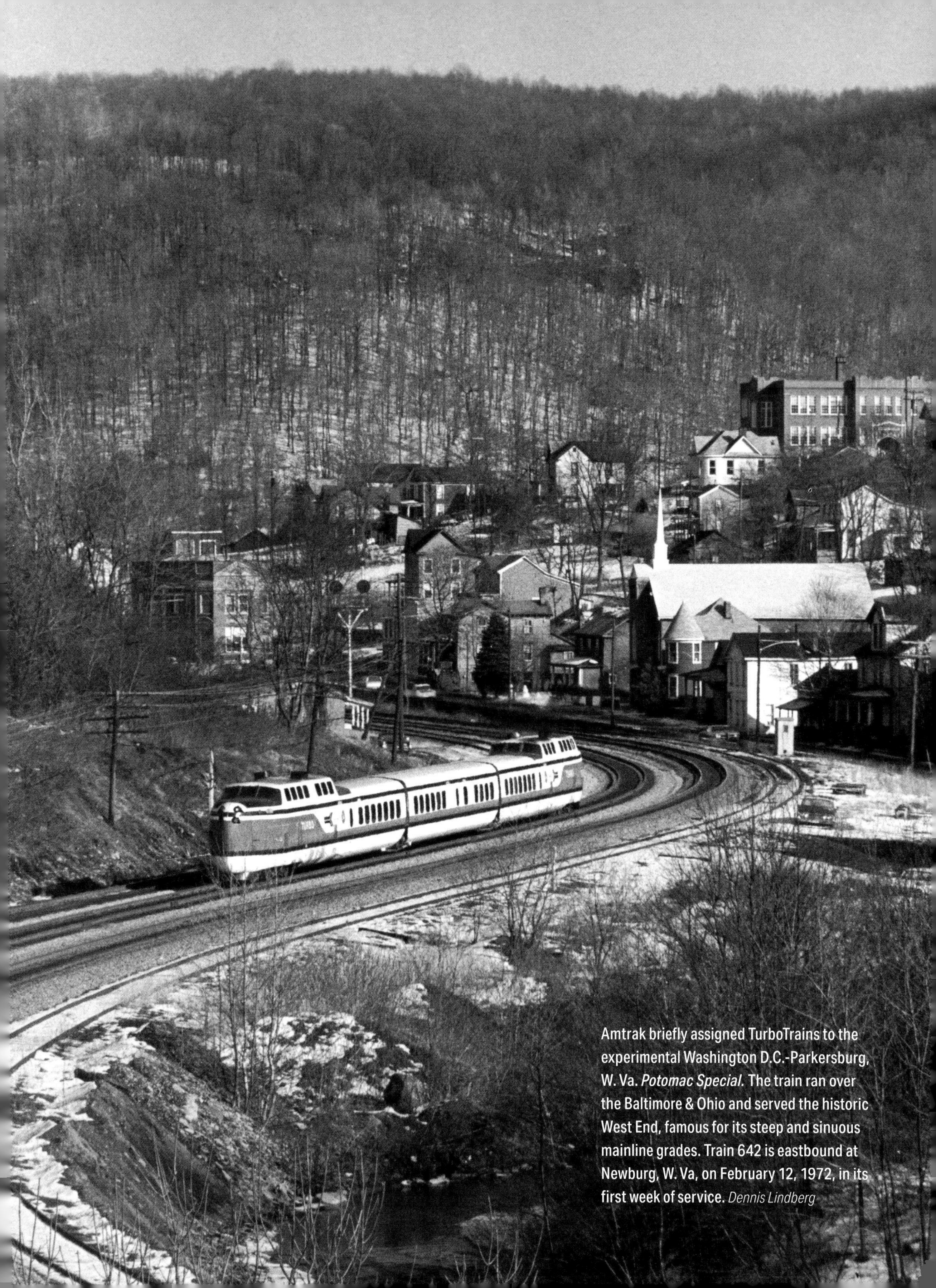

Amtrak briefly assigned TurboTrains to the experimental Washington D.C.-Parkersburg, W. Va. *Potomac Special.* The train ran over the Baltimore & Ohio and served the historic West End, famous for its steep and sinuous mainline grades. Train 642 is eastbound at Newburg, W. Va, on February 12, 1972, in its first week of service. *Dennis Lindberg*

Amtrak eventually expanded its United Aircraft TurboTrains to five-unit trainsets with the addition of two intermediate cars. This is a trailing view of train No. 151, the *Flying Yankee* (Boston-New York), at the west end of the New Haven station at 9:38 a.m. on February 12, 1976. With a UA TurboTrain's faster speed, Train 151's Monday-Thursday express run was accomplished in just four hours, 18 minutes.
George W. Kowanski

In Amtrak's early years, Metroliners featured prominently in its advertising and public timetables and by 1972 the trains were carrying more than 2 million passengers annually.

By 1973, Amtrak needed a new passenger fleet and worked with Budd to adapt the basic design of the Metroliner into a stand-alone locomotive-hauled passenger car: Amfleet (see Chapter 7). However, difficulties remained with the original trains and in 1975, Amtrak initiated a program to overhaul the Metroliner cars. By 1978, 34 of 61 cars had been improved, which included adding a hump to the top of the cars for dynamic braking grids and related cooling ventilation. The remaining cars retained their as-built appearance.

Amtrak wanted a better solution for powering high-speed service, which ultimately resulted in the AEM7 locomotive fleet (Chapter 6). At the end of October 1981, AEM7s hauling specially assigned Amfleet cars assumed operation of *Metroliner* schedules, while the

original trains were reassigned as *Capitoliners* on the Philadelphia-Harrisburg Keystone Corridor.

The Metroliner cars were Amtrak's only electric multiple-unit cars. In 1987, Amtrak's Wilmington, Del., shops began converting Metroliner MP85E4 coaches into "control coaches" (cab-control cars) to lead push-pull consists of the similar-looking Amfleet cars. Since the early 1970s, commuter rail operators had made good use of push-pull trainsets, which greatly simplify operations at end terminals. Initially, Amtrak assigned control coaches to *San Diegan* service between Los Angeles and San Diego, sending the old Metroliner cars about as far from their old home territory as possible within the Amtrak network. In 1989, more Metroliner cars were converted, at first for Atlantic City service. Ultimately, 29 former Metroliner coaches were converted (and reassigned into the 9600 series).

A few Metroliner cars were rebuilt as coaches (without cabs), while some

Amtrak's Turboliners represented a 1970s vision of modern railroading. In November 1986, this Rohr Turboliner was just 10 years old when pictured departing Rochester, N.Y., for the run eastward over the Water Level Route to New York's Grand Central Terminal. Note the vastly different styling of the Rohr trainset compared to the UA TurboTrain. *Brian Solomon*

others were transformed for specialized applications. Snack bar-coach 863 became a control-cab conference car, and another car was sold to the DOT to become track geometry car T-16. Car 884, among the coach conversions, was later transformed into No. 10005, which carried ground-penetrating radar and catenary measurement instruments. Many of the remaining unmodified snack bar-coaches and Metro Club cars were scrapped.

By 2024, surviving control coaches had served twice as long in their reconfigured service than they had as self-propelled high-speed trains. They have worked a variety of services including *Hiawatha* and *Wolverine* trains out of Chicago; the Washington D.C.-St. Albans, Vt., *Vermonter* during the years when the train required a reverse move at Palmer, Mass.; as 400-series, two-car shuttle trains between Springfield, Mass., and New Haven; and on electric locomotive-powered *Keystones* between New York, Philadelphia, and Harrisburg, Pa.

These functional antiques have spanned the entire Amtrak lineage and are among the oldest revenue equipment on the network. Metroliner snack bar-coach 960 is among Amtrak equipment displayed at the Railroad Museum of Pennsylvania in Strasburg.

United Aircraft TurboTrain: Nos. 50-57

United Aircraft's innovative TurboTrain was an outgrowth of the development of lightweight articulated trains in the 1950s. New Haven had been a customer for the early Spanish-designed Talgo trains, which unfortunately suffered from poor performance and didn't last

This artist's rendering depicts the vision for one of the Rohr Turboliners (RTL) before the trains were completed and ready for service. *Amtrak*

long in service. United Aircraft had expressed interested in advanced train design, and moved to develop a new line of trains as result of President Lyndon Johnson's High Speed Ground Transportation Act of 1965, which made federal funds available to for high-speed train development.

For this, UA worked with Alan R. Cripe, who was closely involved with Chesapeake & Ohio's lightweight Train-X in the 1950s, which benefited from an advanced pendular suspension system. This technology was blended with aircraft-style lightweight articulated train bodies of welded aluminum with gas-turbine propulsion.

Although several manufacturers — notably GE — had dabbled with gas-turbine power for heavy rail applications, the adaptation of gas-turbine engines on a super high-speed passenger train was novel concept. The result was UA's futuristic lightweight aerodynamic TurboTrain. United progressed from design to a demonstration prototype in just two years, with the first train making its debut in 1967. The three-car trainset was built by the Surface Transportation Systems Subdivision of Sikorsky Aircraft Division of United Aircraft Corporation, and assembled by Pullman-Standard in Chicago.

A power car was positioned at each end, with a total of four Pratt & Whitney 400-hp ST-6B aircraft turbines delivering power through direct-gear drive, plus a fifth turbine used to generate head-end power (HEP).

To provide the best aerodynamics, the body of the train was designed using a wind tunnel. This reduced wind resistance for greater speed potential

A French-built RTG Turboliner that had worked train No. 307 from Chicago rests after arriving beneath St. Louis Union Station's cavernous train shed. It's 1:09 p.m. on Oct. 18, 1975; Amtrak would abandon the station in 1978. *George W. Kowanski*

Amtrak
61

A Metroliner appeared on the cover of Amtrak's Jan. 6, 1974, New York-Philadelphia public timetable. This train was the most modern and fastest in Amtrak's fleet. Fifty years later, a few of these classic cars survive in revenue service as push-pull control coaches.
Richard Jay Solomon collection

and also contributed to a futuristic appearance that appealed to a general public thrilled by space-age developments. Despite using elevated dome sections at each end of the consist, the train's cars were nearly three feet shorter than conventional passenger cars and had a lower center of gravity.

The three-car set was 203 feet long, weighed just 105 tons (much less than traditional passenger cars), and had seats for 144 passengers. The combination of wind-resistant bodies, guided axles to reduce wheel/rail resistance in curves, low center of gravity, and pendular suspension — along with the turbine propulsion — enabled the TurboTrain to accelerate rapidly and operate through curves 36% to 46% faster than conventional equipment by minimizing the effects of centrifugal forces on passengers.

The hope was that TurboTrain would offer fast, comfortable service on existing tracks without the need to radically alter rail infrastructure. Its initial intended application was for the New Haven's Boston-New York run, which suffered from a relatively sinuous profile and would benefit from the train's innovative design. The TurboTrain demonstrated its state-of-the-art technology during a November 1967 press run on the Pennsylvania between New Brunswick and Trenton, N.J., when a prototype train hit the astounding top speed of 170.8 mph.

TurboTrain was developed in parallel with Budd's Metroliner, and it was hoped that together these new trains would rejuvenate passenger service on the busy Northeast Corridor. By the time they were ready for commercial service, the New Haven and Pennsylvania were both part of the newly formed Penn Central system, and a goal was that TurboTrain would allow railroads to effectively compete with airlines in short intercity corridors.

Under Penn Central, the TurboTrain debuted in Boston-Grand Central service on April 8, 1969. Despite its super-fast design speed, it was limited to a conservative 100 mph in revenue service to conform with limitations of existing infrastructure and signaling. Still, this trimmed Boston-New York travel time to just 3 hours, 39 minutes.

Amtrak inherited PC's TurboTrains and the prerogative to operate high-speed rail service in the Northeast. By the time Amtrak began operations in May 1971, TurboTrain schedules had been rerouted in New York from Grand Central to Penn Station to allow connections with Metroliner electric services to Washington.

During Amtrak's early years, TurboTrain was at the forefront of American train development. It represented a bold vision for the future and a contrast from Amtrak's tired inherited equipment from the 1940s and 50s that represent the bulk of its fleet. TurboTrain images often appeared in advertisements, timetables, and promotional brochures. Shortly after Amtrak assumed operations, a freshly painted TurboTrain made a 31-state tour. In early 1972, Amtrak assigned one set to work the Baltimore & Ohio between Washington, D.C., and Parkersburg, W.Va. However, the train didn't perform well on this route, which was known for having some of the steepest mainline grades in the East.

Under Amtrak, TurboTrain power cars were numbered 50-53, with coaches numbered in the 70 series. In 1972, Amtrak expanded its UA TurboTrains from three to five cars. In 1973, it aimed to acquire two additional sets

from Canadian National; unfortunately, during an acceptance trial one of the trains was destroyed in an accident. In February 1974, the surviving former CN train (Nos. 56-57) traveled west to Chicago, where it tested on the former Alton Route to St. Louis. It later returned east, and by late 1974, Amtrak scheduled two daily New York-Boston round trips using TurboTrains.

While these innovative trains captured the public's attention and imagination, the ride quality wasn't always the best, especially when navigating terminal trackage at slow speeds, and they were louder than conventional cars. TurboTrains also suffered a variety of technical problems that required abnormally high amounts of maintenance and lower-than-normal availability.

The trains' future was sealed when United Aircraft exited the railcar business in 1974. In 1976, new EMD F40PH diesels hauling Budd-built, HEP-equipped Amfleet passenger cars offered more effective and more reliable transportation. After these were assigned to Boston-New York-Washington service, Amtrak quietly withdrew UA TurboTrains from service in September that year. The trains were stored for several years before formal retirement in 1979, and were ultimately scrapped in the early 1980s.

In 1987, Amtrak rebuilt three of its French RTG Turboliners, which included fitting them with streamlined nose sections similar to those used by the Rohr Turboliners. These were reassigned to Empire service and based out of Albany-Rensselaer, N.Y. Here RTGII power car 68 rests during a Poughkeepsie, N.Y., station stop on July 29, 1988.

Brian Solomon

Turboliners — ANF RTG Trains: Nos. 58-69

Following Amtrak's start-up, it faced a need for new, comparatively fast rolling stock offering a modern image that would excite the traveling public. However, at the time domestic suppliers didn't have reliable, state-of-the-art long-distance train designs that could be built and delivered quickly. Amtrak therefore looked to Europe, where decades of progressive rail passenger development had produced a variety of modern trains.

In 1972, Amtrak ordered a pair of five-car RTG (Ram Turbine Gas) turbo trains from French manufacturer ANF. These were essentially a stock design that was readily adapted for North American service. Technologically similar to UA's TurboTrain, the ANF trains shared a similar configuration, as they were doubled-ended (a cab and turbine power car at each end). Each featured a

1,140-hp Turbomeca Tumo III gas turbine that engaged driving wheels through a Voith torque-converter hydraulic transmission. They were shipped from France on the *Atlantic Cognac* and delivered in 1973.

Power cars were numbered 60-63, and the trainsets were dressed in a flashy version Amtrak's early standard Phase I livery with white bodies and broad, bold Amtrak red and heritage blue striping separated by a white pinstripe running the length of the train and wrapping around the ends. The Arrow logo with blue Amtrak lettering was on the sides of each power car. The undercarriage was black.

The trains had initial success, leading Amtrak to order another four trainsets which were built in February 1975. These power cars were numbered 58-59 and 64-69. Amtrak assigned the ANF-RTG turbos to Chicago, where they were maintained at a specialized shop

In early 1996, several years after it was withdrawn from service, this ANF RTG Turboliner awaits its end at an Indiana scrap yard.
Scott Muskopf

at Brighton Park. They were initially assigned to Chicago-St. Louis service and later served a prominent stint on the Chicago-Milwaukee corridor.

In 1981, the ANF trains were taken out of service and stored. In 1987, three of the trains were rebuilt as RTG-II and fitted with new cab ends that matched the profile of the later Rohr RTL sets (see the next section) and reassigned to Empire Corridor service. In 1994, a serious fire involving RTG-II power car 64 contributed to the decision to withdraw the RTG-II turbos from regular service.

Empire Corridor (RTL) Turboliners

Amtrak's success with the RTG turbo trains in the 1970s led it to work with a domestic aerospace supplier, Rohr Industries of Chula Vista, Calif., for seven

similar five-car sets known as Turboliners. They were built under license from ANF in 1976-1977 for the estimated cost of $32 million. Although a relatively obscure name in railroad manufacturing, Rohr had also built modern rapid-transit vehicles for the then-new Bay Area Rapid Transit and Washington, D.C. Metro in the early 1970s.

The plan was to use them for Boston-New York service on the Northeast Corridor, but the arrival of F40PH diesels and Amfleet cars proved a better fit for through Boston-Washington trains. As a result, the Rohr Turboliners were assigned to New York's Empire Corridor, a route previously identified as an ideal service for these trains. Power cars were numbered 150-163.

The RTL Turboliners featured a decidedly different cab profile with a steeply sloped streamlined front end that gave crews a better forward view and superior collision protection. Other differences included standard end couplers and a secondary propulsion system using traction motors powered off lineside electrified third rail to enable operation into New York City terminals. Initially these served Grand Central, but after 1991 they reached Penn

← ↑ The lone RTL II Turboliner races toward Poughkeepsie past Bannerman on September 4, 1997, in coming (left) and going (above) views. This set, including power cars 151 and 159, was rebuilt from one of the Rohr Industries RTL trainsets. Notably, it featured more powerful turbines, an interior makeover, and a unique paint scheme. Work on the power cars was performed under contract by Morrison-Knudsen at the former Erie Railroad shops in Hornell, N.Y. *Two photos: Brian Solomon*

Station via a new connection off the old West Side line.

On September 19, 1976, these trains made their debut at Albany-Rensselaer station, located near the shops where they were based and maintained. Until the mid-1990s the RTLs worked many of the Empire Corridor services. While primarily focused on the New York-Albany run, where they could race up to 110 mph, the RTLs also worked west to Buffalo and Niagara Falls on the former New York Central Water Level route, and for a few years served on the *Adirondack* that ran over Delaware & Hudson north of Schenectady to Montreal.

The arrival of new Genesis dual-mode P32ACDMs beginning in 1995 allowed Amtrak to scale back services with the two-decade-old RTLs. However, Amtrak contracted Morrison-Knudsen to rebuild a single Rohr Turboliner at Hornell, N.Y. The work was completed by MK's railcar-building successor, Amerail. For several years the rebuilt train, described as an RTL-II and wearing a distinctive red, black, and gray livery, remained the lone turbo in Empire Corridor service.

During the X-2000's Northeast Corridor demonstration period in Spring 1993, Amtrak assigned a pair of specially painted Turboliner power cars to lead the train on the non-electrified portion of the route between Boston and New Haven. The Turboliners and ABB's X-2000 are seen at New Haven, Conn., on May 7, 1993. *Walter E. Zullig, Jr.*

Last of the Turboliners

New York State retained its involvement with the RTL trains, and in the late-1990s it came to an arrangement with Amtrak to rebuild and update all seven RTL trains as RTL-IIIs for fast (up to 125 mph) service on the Empire Corridor. The New York DOT financed the project, which unfortunately suffered from a variety of complications and setbacks.

Ultimately three trains were rebuilt by SuperSteel in Schenectady, N.Y. Work included structural remanufacturing, traction system upgrades, a redesigned interior, and better engine airflow. Two sets were ready for service by 2003 and dressed in a modern livery adapted from Amtrak's Phase V scheme, similar to that applied to Acela Express HSTs.

New York and Amtrak faced decidedly different visions for the unusual RTL-IIIs, and by September 2004 the trains were withdrawn from service again and returned to storage. The remaining four sets did not complete the rebuild program and were ultimately scrapped.

2038
AMTRAK
acela
2038

Boston-bound *Acela Express* Train 2166, led by power car 2038, approaches its maximum authorized speed of 150 mph as it flashes through Mansfield, Mass., on June 19, 2015. The electrified Acela trains began testing in the late 1990s and entered revenue service on December 10, 2000; Amtrak's initial goal was for Acela Express to replace Metroliner high-speed services, which since the early 1980s had operated with AEM7s and Amfleet cars. *Brian Solomon*

From LRC to Acela

Post-turbo-era self-contained cars led to modern trainsets

Following the mixed results of the UA, RTG, and RTL turbos, during the 1980s and 1990s Amtrak imported several trains for experimental service and to gauge public perception of other modern train designs. Between June 1980 and April 1982, Amtrak leased from the Canadian government a pair of Bombardier-built Light-Rapid-Comfortable (LRC) tilting trains for revenue service between New York and Boston. Bombardier, which had acquired Alco's one-time Canadian affiliate Montreal Locomotive Works, continued to advance MLW's products.

Bombardier LRC

Each of the two five-car LRC trains was powered by a low-profile, wedge-nosed Bombardier power car-locomotive (Amtrak 38 and 39, variously described as model LRC-2/M429LRC), powered by an advanced version of the Alco-MLW 16-cylinder 251 diesel. The trains were painted for Amtrak with largely white bodies and blue underbodies separated by red and white striping. This distinctive livery earned them the nickname "ice cream trains." Under wire, west of New Haven, Amtrak's LRC trains were hauled by electrics to reach New York's Penn Station. While the vir-

tues of the Alco 251 diesels were soon forgotten, the LRC's active tilting system had caught Amtrak's attention.

In conjunction with the train's two-year trial service in the United States, a joint DOT/Federal Railroad Administration (FRA)/Amtrak project contracted ENSCO, Inc., to perform a series of detailed repetitive comparison tests between Amfleet equipment and the LRC to examine the effectiveness of the LRC's tilting system. In its 1982 report, "High Cant Deficiency Test of the LRC Train" (comparing to the AEM7 locomotive and the Amcoach), the FRA published the results of these tests and the advantages of LRC's tilting technology. "Increasing the speed of passenger trains in existing curves has been proposed as an alternative to changing curve radii for the purpose of reducing trip times on the Northeast Corridor … Tests were performed on the advanced LRC train with banking coaches and the modern but conventional AEM7 Locomotive and Amcoach.

"The criteria concerning safety against vehicle overturning set the cant deficiency limits for all four vehicles, and the crosswind allowance set lower limits for coaches than locomotives. A typical curve limited to 60 mph by the current 3" cant deficiency limit could be negotiated by the LRC train at up to approximately 79 mph (9" cant deficiency) while holding the steady state lateral acceleration below the AAR ride comfort criterion." Mainline tests were conducted on a heavily curved portion of the NEC between New Haven and Providence, as well as under wire between New York and Washington, and on the Harrisburg Line between Philadelphia and Harrisburg. Amtrak returned its LRC locomotives and cars to Canada in Spring 1982.

VIA Rail later acquired the LRC rolling stock formerly leased to Amtrak, and assigned some of these cars to its portion of the jointly operated Chicago-Toronto *International,* which resulted in this unusual equipment running all the way to Chicago Union Station behind VIA Rail F40PH-2s.

Swedish X2000 and German ICE-1

A decade after the LRC tests, Amtrak's renewed interest in existing high-speed train designs resulted in extensive examination and consideration by the

← Amtrak 39, one of two leased Bombardier LRC-2 locomotives, leads Amfleet I cars on *The Shoreliner,* train No. 151 (Boston-New York Penn Station) at New Haven, Conn., on November 22, 1980. The LRC-2 locomotives were designed to operate with Bombardier's Light, Rapid, Comfortable (LRC) tilting trainsets. Built in 1980, these unusual diesels spent two years in Amtrak service. *Walter E. Zullig, Jr.*

Setting a precedent for an electrically hauled Bombardier tilting train, GE E60CH 973 leads one of two borrowed Bombardier LRC sets working as *The Shoreliner* on the former New Haven Railroad on May 25, 1981. *Walter E. Zullig, Jr.*

FRA. Some of FRA's findings were published in a December 1990 report on the Swedish X2000 train that offered this insight, "The use of various high-speed rail technologies for high-speed ground transportation in the United States may become a reality within the next few years. As a result of these developments, there is a need to review the safety of those high-speed rail systems that may utilize differing equipment and operating procedures from those currently employed in the United States."

During 1992 and 1993, Amtrak imported and tested two of the latest European high-speed trains for testing on the Northeast Corridor. It also dispatched these state-of-the art trains on nationwide tours to help encourage public interest in modern high-speed rail. First to arrive was an example of the Swedish State Railways (SJ) X2000 high-speed train built by ABB. This six-car, stainless-steel body-tilting train looked like a natural successor to the original Metroliner cars. It was a push-pull design with a power car at one end, a bistro-snack car, three intermediate coaches, and a coach/cab-control car at the far end.

Unlike the passive pendular tilt system employed by the UA TurboTrain (and Talgo trains described in Chapter 6), the X2000 used a steerable truck and an active tilting system, described by the DOT/FRA in its December 1990 report, "Car-body tilt is actuated in response to controller-transmitted commands … in this design, measurements are made of various system conditions such as the lateral acceleration, from which this information is then processed by the controller to activate the appropriate car-body tilt." Compared to passive tilting systems, this was more complex, but offered a distinct advantage, since "the tilt configuration can be designed to limit the

shift in the car-body center of gravity which would reduce wheel unloading." The passenger cars tilt, but the power car does not.

In its review of the X2000's developmental history, the DOT/FRA explained interest in this advanced train compared with other European innovations. "By utilizing existing track with certain upgrades of the track structure and signaling system, SJ has chosen to trade off higher maximum speeds, 200km/h vs. 300 km/h (125 mph vs 186 mph), that would be attainable with other current high-speed train technology such as the French TGV developed by French National Railways, SNCF, and the German Federal Railway, DB, for lower track costs.

"Although both the TGV and ICE technologies can operate on existing non-high-speed rail lines, operation at their maximum revenue speeds requires a track structure that is more limited in its maximum curvatures and that must be completely grade separated at all crossings with other modes. This more extensive rebuilding of existing track, or in some cases, completely new rights-of-way, is required for the TGV and ICE to reach their full speed potential."

As built for service in Sweden, the X2000 complied with International

A six-car Swedish ABB-built X2000 streamlined stainless-steel tilting train-set arrives in the United States via the port of Baltimore, where it's being unloaded from the *Faust* on October 20, 1992.
Dan Cupper

"Amtrak's Acela Express was developed as a successor to the popular and successful Metroliner service on the Northeast Corridor."

Union of Railways (UIC) buff strength standards; however, those were less demanding than those recommended by the Association of American Railroads, which was a complicating factor with importing existing European trains for regular service. The FRA detailed these considerations in a 1990 report, noting that the train met the UIC buff strength requirements of 203 metric tons (448,000 pounds) of force, but that an imported production train would require meeting the U.S. requirement of 363 metric tons (800,000 pounds) applied to the centerline of draft.

The borrowed SJ X2000 set was imported through Baltimore, Md., on October 20, 1992, then set up at Washington Union Station where it was put on public display. The train was lettered for Amtrak. It entered revenue demonstration service on the Northeast Corridor in February 1993 and spent 3 months working under wire before being sent on a nationwide tour.

In June, a Siemens-built Deutsche Bahn (German Railways) ICE-1 train arrived in the United States. This toured first, hauled by experimental F69PHACs (with Siemens AC propulsion; see Chapter 6), before entering overhead-wire electric service on the NEC in October. This train had power cars at each end, with six intermediate cars including a bistro-snack car and an elegant full-service diner.

Both trains were returned overseas after their demonstrations. While neither the ICE nor X2000 were selected for Amtrak's long-term applications, both trains helped demonstrate the value of modern high-speed designs and played important roles in improving rail service on the Northeast Corridor, including raising maximum speeds, employing active tilting systems, and bringing to fruition the long-held dream of extending overhead electrification from New Haven to Boston.

IC3 Flexliner

During 1996 and 1997, Amtrak participated in a series of demonstrations using two imported Danish IC3 Flexliner diesel multiple-unit sets. These trainsets, lettered for Amtrak, worked established schedules on the Chicago-Milwaukee *Hiawatha,* St. Louis-Kansas City runs, and various demonstrations in Minnesota, Oregon, and California (including *San Diegan* service).

The innovative Flexliner design has been credited to Niels Tongaard Nielson and Jens Nielson. It was a distinctive, lightweight bidirectional articulated three-unit self-propelled train. As built it was capable of speeds up to 112 mph with seats for 140 passengers. It was noteworthy for its ability to be automatically joined and separated quickly. Control compartments were designed to fold out of the way after the trains were joined to enable passengers to move freely between cars. This gave the compact train great comfort, versatility and flexibility — qualities inferred by its name.

Each trainset had power cars at both ends with an unpowered center car between. Bodies were aluminum with distinctive rubber padded ends to aid in safe coupling. They were built by Adtranz (a joint venture of ABB and Daimler Benz, later acquired by Bombardier). The Danish national railroad (DSB) made excellent use of these trains in regional passenger service starting around 1990. Amtrak was interested in testing these trains as an economical, fuel-efficient option for medium-distance service, but didn't make a long-term commitment to them.

For three months beginning on February 1, 1993, the borrowed ABB X2000 worked in scheduled Amtrak service. On April 9, 1993, the X2000 trainset works as Metroliner Train 223 on the former New Haven at Mamaroneck, N.Y. *Walter E. Zullig, Jr.*

Bombardier-Alstom Acela Express HST: Nos. 2000-2039

Amtrak's Acela Express was developed as the successor to the popular and successful *Metroliner* service aimed at improving high-speed rail transportation on the Boston-New York-Washington Northeast Corridor. Amtrak literature explains that the name "Acela" was derived from the combination of "acceleration" and "excellence," while the original Acela logo is an adaption of a sea turtle fin that also offers an abstraction of railroad tracks.

Introduction of *Acela Express* service (initially the premium level of Acela fast electric services, including locomotive-hauled *Acela* regional trains) coincided with completion of electrification between Boston and New Haven. Significant track upgrades on key portions of the line allow for safe maximum authorized speeds up to 150 mph. These improvements enabled through overhead electric operations between Boston and Washington while eliminating the time-consuming engine change at New Haven. Faster train speeds and the high-speed trainset's tilting design shortened travel times and allowed Amtrak to better compete with other transportation options.

Acela Express service made its debut using new purpose-built Bombardier-Alstom High Speed Trainsets (HSTs) that immediately became synonymous with the Acela brand. Although the Acela hardware and branding are closely intertwined, as with the Metroliner it is important to distinguish between the equipment and the service that it provided. Development of HST was an outgrowth of Am-

On its tour of the Midwest, the ABB-built X2000 passes Roosevelt Road in Chicago on its way to Detroit on July 22, 1993. The electrically powered train was hauled by F40PH diesels on this leg of its North American journey. Rows of bilevel Metra commuter cars rest in the background. *Mike Abalos*

Officials and members of the media tour the dining car on the imported ICE train during a press run on September 14, 1993. This modern train spent two months in revenue service on the Northeast Corridor beginning in October 1993.
Walter E. Zullig, Jr.

trak's experiments with the German ICE and Swedish X2000 high speed trains in the early 1990s, as well as its earlier experiences with Talgo and LRC trains, as well as the original Metroliner cars and the United Aircraft TurboTrain.

Many observers familiar with the X2000 argued that from a technological perspective, that technology offered nearly an ideal solution for Amtrak's high-speed service. Former Amtrak president David Gunn summed up the X2000 by saying, "it was reliable, simple, proven." But he explained that Amtrak sought an alternative solution "… because the Canadian government is great at providing financing."

Acela Express HSTs were built by a consortium of Alstom and Bombardier and employed a unique combination of European and Canadian technology. This melded Alstom's high-speed propulsion system engineered for the French high-speed TGV with the active tilting mechanism developed by Bombardier for Canada's Light-Rapid-Comfortable (LRC) trains. In this arrangement, only the passenger cars tilt, to reduce the effect of centrifugal forces for greater passenger comfort when taking curves at high speeds.

Between 1998 and 2000, 20 of these trainsets were built for Amtrak. They were assembled at Barre, Vt., with final setup work performed in New York. The train spent months undergoing tests. Before the new train could enter service, a design flaw was discovered that made news: The passenger cars were four inches too wide, which meant there was concern for a potential collision in the unlikely situation where trains passing in a tight curve simultaneously suffered serious tilt-mechanism failure. The solution prevented the trains from taking maximum advantage of the tilting systems.

Amtrak began its long-awaited electrified service to Boston in January 2000, at first operating just a few of the numerous Northeast Direct trains behind AEM7 electric locomotives. The Acela Express HSTs continued undergoing trials on various portions of the route while the sets were debugged. *Acela Express* service made its debut under overcast skies on December 10, 2000, with the first public run from Washington to Boston led by power car 2009. It was the dawn of a new era for American high-speed rail.

While the new trains were marketed as *Acela Express*, some traditional locomotive-hauled Amfleet trains were called *Acela Regional*. This proved confusing and after a few years the Acela Regional brand was replaced by the new Northeast Regional brand for the Amfleet trains. This left the Acela name strictly for the premium express services provided by the purpose-built HSTs. From the beginning, *Acela Express* trains only offered first-class and business-class accommodations. Coach passengers had a choice of regional trains.

The intent was for Acela service to replace the popular Metroliner service — which at the time was largely provided by upscaled Amfleet cars hauled by AEM7s on fast, limited-stop schedules — but there was considerable overlap between the two brands. By Spring 2001, as more HSTs entered service, Amtrak began replacing *Metroliner* schedules with additional *Acela Express* runs. The phasing out of Metroliner was disrupted in 2002 and 2005 when the HST sets were temporarily withdrawn to repair defects. The last *Metroliner* schedule ran in October 2006.

The HST trains are arranged in 20 semipermanently coupled trainsets, with a locomotive power car at each end. Most sets have operated with six intermediate cars in a typical consist as follows: end coach, coach, café, two coaches, and a first-class car. Amtrak's procedures state that two trainsets may be coupled to form a single consist, while up to four coaches may be added to a fixed set. Power cars are numbered 2000-2039, first-class cars 3200-3219, café cars 3300-3319, end coach cars 3400-3419, and coach cars 3500-3559.

The power cars use a modern polyphase propulsion system. These draw high-voltage AC power from overhead wire via a single-arm pantograph at any of the three standard voltage/frequency combinations used on the Northeast Corridor (described in Chapter 6). Power passes through a

The German ICE train pauses at New Haven, Conn., during a demonstration run on September 14, 1993. *Walter E. Zullig, Jr.*

main circuit breaker and then to the main transformer, which has two primary windings. Transformer windings are connected in parallel when the overhead voltage is between 12-12.5 kV, and in series when the overhead voltage is 25 kV. When making the transition between standard power supplies, the switch from parallel to series is made by an automatically controlled, motor-driven tap changer. The main transformer converts the AC power to high-voltage DC (nominally 2,750 volts) which is fed to a pair of high-voltage motor inverters that convert the output back to a form of AC power using gate-turnoff thyristors to power traction motors. Each inverter supplies two traction motors.

A third inverter is used to supply high-voltage AC for auxiliary equipment including a head-end power transformer that steps current down for train heating, lighting, and other onboard systems. Up to 1,000 kW of HEP is supplied to the train at Amtrak's on-board electrical standard voltage/frequency (three-phase, 480 volts AC at

60 Hz). The power cars are designed with regenerative braking that can feed current from traction motors back to the catenary, or function as rheostatic braking (dynamic braking) with current directed to brake resistor grids that dissipate energy.

Each power car has four traction motors and can supply a maximum of 6,169 hp continuously (12,338 hp for the train). This exceptional high horsepower-to-weight ratio allows rapid acceleration and continuous high speed. Starting tractive effort is calculated at 49,400 pounds with a maximum starting current draw of 690 amps.

According to manufacturer specifications, the power cars weigh 200,000 pounds each, with maximum axle weight of 50,750 pounds. Power cars are just over 69 feet long and 14'-2" tall to the roof; a fully extended pantograph reaches 25'-2" above the rail). The wheels are 40" in diameter and traction motors are a three-phase, four-pole, induction type for asynchronous AC; the gear ratio is 71:23.

Passenger cars are 87 feet long and

On April 30, 1997, an imported Danish-built IC3 Flexliner diesel-multiple unit working as Train 301 (westbound *Kansas City Mule*) departs its station stop at Kirkwood, Mo. During 1996 and 1997, two imported IC3 sets made demonstration runs in various Amtrak services. *Scott Muskopf*

➡ ⬇ Coming (right) and going (below) views at West Haven, Conn., show an Acela Express High-Speed Trainset led by power car 2017, with 2036 on the trailing end, on February 7, 2014. Twenty of these distinctive trains were built by the Bombardier-Alstom consortium for Amtrak high-speed service. *Two photos: Brian Solomon*

weigh between 127,000 and 129,000 pounds, depending on configuration. Coach cars were designed with 65 seats, first-class cars have 44 seats, and a typical six-car train offers a total of 304 seats. A full trainset with power cars stretches 663 feet long and weighs about 1,171,000 pounds (585 tons).

Amtrak required 14 HSTs to fulfill normal weekday *Acela Express* schedules in 2004. Typically, an additional two trains were maintained serviceable for standby service, one at each end of electrified territory, to cover the schedule in the event of train failure or an extremely late-running incoming train.

Traveling on an Acela HST is an exhilarating experience, allowing passengers the thrill of rapid, smooth acceleration, high-speed running, and the mild sensation of active tilting in curves.

Acela next generation: Nos. 2100-2155

In 2016, Amtrak ordered 28 new high-speed trainsets from Alstom to replace the original HSTs that had worked *Acela Express* services since 2000. The new trains are an adaptation of Alstom's successful Avelia trains, which incorporate the Tiltronix tilting system that evolved from the Fiat Ferroviaria Pendolino system developed in Italy, which is in use on trains in a dozen nations around the world. The car shells/bodies are patterned after the Italian AGV car type.

Design details were developed in a partnership between Alstom, Amtrak, and the Federal Railroad Administration. Although the train's fundamental technology is largely adapted from modern European designs, 95% of the

On September 28, 2020, a vision of the future blitzed eastbound through Levittown, Pa., on Train 874 en route to Boston for high-speed testing. These modern high-speed trains were initially called Acela 21 and Avelia Liberty, but are now simply described as the "New Acela" or "Acela Next Generation." After more than four years since the equipment's early trials, it was hoped that the new trains would enter revenue service by early 2025. *Patrick Yough*

acela
AMTRAK
SEPTA
Levittown
Trains to Center City Philadelphia
Daily Parking

A Washington D.C.-bound *Acela Express* has clear signals at Eddystone, Pa., as it races away from the photographer toward the setting sun. Since 2000, Amtrak's Acela Express High-Speed Trainsets have provided premium service on the Boston-New York-Washington Northeast Corridor. *Brian Solomon*

components are built in the United States, with final assembly conducted at Alstom's Hornell, N.Y. plant (located on the site of the former Erie Railroad shops). Amtrak had initially considered using a multiple-unit design, where traction motors were distributed throughout the train — as with the original 1960s-era Metroliners — but ultimately settled on a train with a high-horsepower power car at each end of non-powered passenger cars, similar to the original Acela trains.

The new design aims to reduce energy consumption by 15-30% compared to the older trains. The propulsion is a modern AC-DC-AC polyphase system using IGBT-VVF technology. Like Amtrak's other overhead electric locomotives, these are designed to draw current from the three principal voltage/frequency standards employed on the Northeast Corridor between Washington, New York, and Boston.

The design meets FRA's Tier III crash safety standards, and the new trains are lighter, with an axle weight of about 17 tons compared to 23 tons on the original HSTs. Although Avelia trains have a top design speed of 220 mph, Amtrak's top operating speed is 160 mph, which conforms with upgraded track conditions on select portions of the Northeast Corridor. When they enter service the next-gen trainsets will be the fastest regularly scheduled trains in North America.

In their initial configuration, trains will consist of nine unpowered passenger cars with a streamlined 4,700-hp power/control unit at each end, with a total length of 698 feet. Power cars are

numbered 2100-2155. Each set includes a first-class car and a food-service car. The trains are designed for operation with up to 12 cars, giving Amtrak the flexibility to increase capacity without scheduling additional trains.

In the trains' early years of development, construction, and testing, Amtrak literature referred to the new equipment as Acela 21 and Avelia Liberty high-speed trainsets. That branding was eventually dropped, and the trains have since been referred to as simply new Acela trains. A new Acela livery was introduced in 2017 ahead of construction.

The prototype train set was completed at Hornell in early 2019 and completed the first round of testing that August. It was then sent to Pueblo, Colo., to the FRA's Transportation Technology Center in September of that year for advanced testing.

In 2020, road tests began on the Northeast Corridor, with the first train arriving at Boston in September. Initially, it was anticipated that the new trains would make their debut in 2021. However, various problems pushed that target forward, and as of March 2025 the new trains have not yet entered revenue service.

This trailing view of Washington-Boston Acela Express train No. 2150 at New London, Conn., on January 10, 2013, shows the rear power car 2032 with first-class car 3216 immediately ahead of it. *Brian Solomon*

1437
Amtrak

CHAPTER 3

Heritage diesels

A rainbow variety of inherited E and F units were the early face of Amtrak

"Heritage" diesels, those units inherited from other railroads upon Amtrak's startup, served as the backbone of Amtrak's long-distance fleet in its first few years. On a clear mid-1970s morning before the train was converted to head-end-power (HEP) equipment, the eastbound *Broadway Limited* departs Harrisburg, Pa., behind E8A 437 (former Richmond, Fredericksburg & Potomac 1001, later Amtrak 213) and E9B 457 (former Union Pacific 954B). *Dan Cupper*

Amtrak began operations in May 1971 with fleets of secondhand EMD E and F unit diesels dressed in the paint of the Class I railroads from which they were acquired. In their heyday, these handsome streamlined carbody diesels were among the finest passenger motive power in North America. However, by the time Amtrak assumed operation most units had rolled a million or more miles in service, many suffering from age and the effects of intense utilization.

When Amtrak began operations in May 1971, it had adopted the iconic Arrow logo but had no paint scheme. For publicity purposes, former Penn Central E8A 4316 (later Amtrak 322) was decorated in an ad hoc scheme with the Arrow in what has since been ironically described as the "day one scheme." Amtrak introduced its Phase I paint scheme the following year. *Jim Hediger*

Although they were approaching the end of their service lives — and many were suffering from deferred maintenance practices of railroads that were trying to end passenger service and cut costs — Amtrak retained some of these antiques for another decade. The legions of Es and Fs diminished rapidly as new diesels eventually arrived in the form of EMD SDP40Fs and F40PHs and GE P30CHs. The E and F represented the face of Amtrak for many early passengers, but by late 1978 just over 50 active units remained.

EMD E and F units: Nos. 100-499

Prior to Amtrak, EMD E and F unit diesel-electrics were the predominant long-distance passenger locomotives during the post-World War II era. Amtrak inherited 216 E8 and E9 units — representing approximately a third of the total production of those models — and 32 F units (models F7A, F3B, F7B and FP7). Amtrak relied upon these streamlined antiques for the majority of its services outside of electrified territory in the Northeast. The Es all had steam generators, which matched the steam systems of the heritage passenger equipment they pulled.

Amtrak focused on the newest E unit models (E8 and E9), looking for locomotives in the best shape among

what was available. In addition, Amtrak leased a variety of additional F and E units from railroads in the 1970s, especially during its difficult startup years (these included some E7s, an earlier model that Amtrak did not own directly). When Amtrak assumed operation of Southern Railway's *Crescent* in 1979, it briefly operated several of that railroad's classy E8s, still painted cream and green with gold striping.

The Electro-Motive Corporation (after 1940 the Electro-Motive Division of General Motors, or simply EMD) E unit line was the direct outgrowth of the power cars used on early diesel-electric streamlined trains of the mid-1930s, and were specifically developed for fast long-distance passenger service. Baltimore & Ohio, Santa Fe, and Union Pacific were the earliest operators of this streamlined carbody type.

The E unit rode on a pair of six-wheel A1A trucks (center axle unpowered), which provided a smooth ride and helped distribute the weight of the locomotive's twin V-12 diesel engines. The Es were built as both A units (with cabs) and B units (cabless). Early E models used 12-cylinder versions of the pioneering Winton diesel, but beginning with model E3, they were built with pairs of EMD 12-567 engines — a design that would evolve to be among the most successful of all time.

After World War II, EMD greatly improved its diesels by refining the component systems. The resulting 2,000-hp model E7 proved the most commercially successful passenger diesel of the postwar period, with more than 500 built from 1945 to 1949. This was supplanted by the more-reliable and more-powerful E8 (2,250 hp) in August 1949, followed by further improvements with model E9 (2,400 hp) in 1954. The E units, as with the company's other diesels, were famous for their power, rugged reliability, and endurance in the most unforgiving operating conditions. EMD eventually sold 421 E8As, 39 E8Bs, 100 E9A, and 40 E9Bs to North American railroads.

By the late 1950s, as railroads were beginning to drastically cut back on passenger service, passenger-diesel production was likewise dropping dramatically. The last of these American classics were completed at EMD's La Grange, Ill., plant in early 1964, built for Union Pacific. The final E built, UP E9A 914, was acquired by Amtrak in 1972, becoming its 419.

The Laredo section of the *Inter-American* approaches a grade crossing protected by a classic wig-wag signal near Temple, Texas, on May 5, 1973. There is little to identify this generic-looking American streamliner except Amtrak 428, former Union Pacific E9A 955.
Joe McMillan

Amtrak owned no E7s, but it did lease some in its early days. Here former Milwaukee Road E9 406 (ex-200C, built in 1956), in Amtrak's Phase I scheme, leads a leased Gulf, Mobile & Ohio E7 on the *Empire Builder* at Milwaukee in the early 1970s. Note the Big Sky Blue ex-Great Northern car trailing.
Earl Thiel

E8A/E8B: 200 and 300 series, 495-499

The E8 was powered by a pair of 12-567B diesels with a combined rating of 2,250 hp. Each engine powered a D15 main generator and D16 alternator to supply power to two D27 traction motors (all upgrades over earlier E units). Several gear ratios were available: 52:25 for a 117-mph maximum; 55:22 for 98 mph; 56:21 for 92 mph; and 57:20 for 85 mph.

Amtrak's fleet of E8s represented 14 original owners, so to avoid operational complications Amtrak standardized on 55:22 gearing for E units. Amtrak's large fleet of E8s were originally numbered 200-374. Some of the E8s in the 200 and 300 series were later renumbered to make room for new F40PHs that arrived beginning in 1976.

New passenger cars were being delivered with electrical head-end power (HEP), so during 1974 and 1975, Amtrak rebuilt five E8As (284, 288, 305, 315, and 317) with HEP and renumbered them 495-499. These were primarily based out of New Haven, Conn., and they eventually outlasted all of Amtrak's steam-generator equipped E units in road service.

In 1983, 498 and 499 were traded to Conrail (for four SW8 switchers), where they became that railroad's executive units 4020 and 4021. These were painted in classic Pullman green and joined former Conrail 4022 in office-car service.

E9A/E9B: 400-472

The E9 was the last E unit model and the final classic EMD streamlined loco-

motive. Although almost identical in outward appearance to the E8, it incorporated a variety of technological improvements associated with EMD's other 9-series diesels (F9, GP9) introduced in 1954. This made it by far the best and most-advanced E unit. The E9 employed pairs of the upgraded 12-567C engine, which at maximum throttle worked at 835 rpm (compared to earlier engines at 800 rpm), and rated at 1,200 hp (2,400 hp total).

Advancement in the engine's cooling circuit improved reliability. Equivalent advancements in the electrical system were reflected in the upgraded D15B main generator and new D37 traction motor, which offered a significant increase in ability to handle short-term motor overload without risk of damage. All of this gave E9s better acceleration, improved ability to handle grades, and improved overall operational characteristics than earlier E units.

In spite of these advancements, E9 sales were slow compared to earlier models. Only 10 railroads purchased them new, as the E9 was only introduced toward the end of the post-World War II passenger train purchasing boom. Amtrak's E9s largely came from Milwaukee Road and Union Pacific, and were numbered in the 400-472 block.

F7/FP7: 100 series

The story of Electro-Motive F units is well known, and the pioneering model FT in 1939 introduced the first powerful road-freight diesel-electric capable of rivaling most modern steam in its ability to reliably move tonnage. The F

Amtrak E8As 283 and 307 wait at New Haven, Conn., to take train No. 170 east to Boston on November 6, 1975. Unit 283 (ex-Penn Central 4275, built as Pennsylvania 5705A in 1952) was a relative rarity: It's one of few E units to receive the Phase II scheme, which featured broad wraparound red and blue stripes with narrow white bands. *George W. Kowanski*

Train No. 62, the *Salt City Express* (Syracuse, N.Y.-New York Grand Central), rolls along the Hudson River approaching Peekskill, N.Y., in November 1974. In the early 1970s, the E8A was the most common model on Amtrak's roster. Former Seaboard Air Line E8A 249 wears fresh Phase I paint. This antique was built in October 1950 and was among a group of similar units acquired by Amtrak from SAL successor Seaboard Coast Line. *George W. Kowanski*

unit differed from the E unit in several key ways, namely in that it had a single 16-cylinder 567 engine and rode on four-wheel trucks with all axles powered. The success of the FT led to extreme popularity of succeeding F unit models once wartime material restrictions were lifted in 1945.

Although primarily a freight locomotive, several railroads opted for steam-generator-equipped F units for passenger service as well (notably Santa Fe, Great Northern, Southern Pacific, and Northern Pacific). They could be geared for higher speeds, and having all axles powered was a benefit on grades.

The FP7 and FP9 models were variations of F units that were specifically designed as passenger locomotives. They featured slightly longer bodies with space for additional water storage to supply steam generators. Several railroads opted for them, especially for assignments on secondary trains.

Amtrak inherited eight F7As (100-107) and seven F3/F7Bs (150-156) from Burlington Northern (which had been created in 1970 from merger

of Chicago, Burlington & Quincy; Great Northern; Northern Pacific; and Spokane, Portland & Seattle), plus 14 FP7s (110-123) and five F7Bs (160-164) from Southern Pacific. Amtrak largely assigned them to its western trains.

Amtrak's F7 and FP7s were among the first locomotives painted in its first standard scheme (Phase I) that emphasized the bold Arrow logo. Except for the FL9s (see the following section), Amtrak's last F units were a pair of former SP FP7s that worked in California and were retired in 1980.

FL9: Nos. 484-491

Electro-Motive's FL9 was a unique model specially developed in the mid-1950s for the New Haven. It was a dual-mode locomotive — a diesel-electric that also had pickup shoes for third-rail electric operation. The FL9 solved several problems for the financially weak New Haven: It allowed for the replacement of antique electric locomotives and World War II-era Alco DL109 diesels, it eliminated the need for engine changes at the limits of overhead electrification (New Haven and Danbury,

Former Union Pacific E9As idle outside the rusting, cavernous steam-era trainshed at St. Louis Union Station in August 1977. Amtrak 419 is former UP 914, the last E built by EMD, delivered in early 1964. Although only seven years old when Amtrak was created, the locomotive unfortunately had an unusually short service life and was scrapped in the early 1980s. Amtrak would leave the station — once the country's largest — in October 1978. *Scott Muskopf*

Amtrak

Amtrak 400 (later renumbered 470) is a former Baltimore & Ohio E9A that was later converted for use as a fuel tender. *Trains Magazine collection*

Conn.), and it overcame challenges with operating diesels in New York City tunnels while complying with unusually light axle-load restrictions.

EMD created the FL9 by adapting its established F unit design to New Haven's requirements. A longer body (58'-8") carried extra internal electrical gear. Along with the dual-mode power system, which could switch between power sources in motion, it needed an unusual wheel arrangement to lower the axle weight, required by the Park Avenue Viaduct in New York City. Instead of the four-wheel Blomberg truck of F units, on the FL9 EMD employed its B Flexicoil truck at the front (to clear the mounting for third-rail shoes) and an A1A Flexicoil (center axle unpowered) truck at the rear to better spread weight.

Two orders of FL9s were delivered to the New Haven — the first in 1956, the second in 1960. As built, these locomotives were rated at 1,750 hp and 1,800 hp respectively. The FL9 became the railroad's dominent passenger locomotive in its final years, and handled the majority of the railroad's intensive long-distance trains on the Shoreline and Springfield routes in its latter days.

New Haven's FL9 fleet went to Penn Central when it absorbed the NH in 1969, and the role and assignment for the FL9s evolved during the PC era. The reduction of long-distance passenger services on former New Haven lines, combined with the preference for through Boston and Springfield trains to be routed via New York's Penn Station instead of Grand Central, resulted in PC shifting E8 diesels and GG1 elec-

trics to New Haven territory. This meant reallocating many FL9s to ex-New York Central routes from Grand Central, allowing for retirement of former NYC third-rail electric locomotives. Part of this was assigning FL9s to work long-distance trains between Grand Central and the end of third rail at Croton-Harmon, with E units working beyond third-rail territory,

In August 1981, an HEP-equipped E8A leads a pair of electric AEM7s eastbound on the former New Haven line across the Hutchinson River at Pelham Bay Park at the Bronx, N.Y. Work on the overhead catenary between Sunnyside Yard and Stamford, Conn., required diesels to lead electric trains through the work zone. *Brian Solomon*

The *Empire Builder* heads westward along the Milwaukee Road at Wauwatosa, Wis., on June 25, 1978. The trailing unit, 675, is former E8A 303, which has been converted into a heater car to supply steam heat to trains led by locomotives (such as these F40PHs) not equipped with steam generators. *George Drury*

The rainbow years: Train No. 9, the westbound *North Coast Hiawatha,* crosses Montana's Homestake Pass on June 20, 1972, behind an A-B-A set of former Northern Pacific passenger-service F7s that are on old home rails. In the lead is Amtrak 103, which was among the earliest diesels painted in Amtrak's first standard scheme, trailed by a B in NP colors and an A in Burlington Northern green. Cars wear a mix of NP, BN, Great Northern, and Amtrak colors. *Philip C. Johnson*

"Although primarily a freight locomotive, several railroads opted for steam-generator-equipped F units for passenger service."

an arrangement that continued into the early Amtrak years.

The creation of Conrail in April 1976 resulted in 12 FL9s being conveyed to Amtrak. Six were assigned to Albany/Rensselaer-based Empire Corridor services. The least-reliable units were cannibalized for parts and then scrapped. In 1979 and 1980, Amtrak contracted Morrison-Knudsen to rebuild and modify its six remaining FL9s, a move that coincided with the

units being renumbered 485-489, plus 491 (later 484).

Rebuilding retained most original equipment, but involved replacement of some key components, such as the traction motors which were upgraded to the more modern D77B. Nominal external modifications reflected changes to facilitate installation of HEP equipment. All six were painted in Amtrak's Phase III livery, similar to contemporary F40PHs. New Haven's

Amtrak FL9 486 — one of six retained for Empire Corridor services — leads Train 63, the westbound *Maple Leaf* (New York-Toronto) near Poughkeepsie, N.Y., on July 9, 1989. The venerable locomotive was built by EMD in 1957 as New Haven No. 2013.
Brian Solomon

➡ **Amtrak's FL9 fleet was given a second major overhaul during 1990-1993 at its Beech Grove shops. This involved replacing or upgrading major mechanical and electrical systems, including swapping the 1950s-era prime mover with EMD 645E power assemblies. There were also a variety of external modifications that included removal of the original vents and access doors on the carbody and relocation of electrical cable receptacles and other equipment. After its second Amtrak-era overhaul, FL9 486 posed outside the Albany-Rensselaer shop on November 15, 1992.**
Brian Solomon

classic Hancock air whistles were replaced with modern five-chime horns. The locomotives were also equipped with high-profile sealed twin-beam headlights, cab-roof strobes, and a red warning strobe on the nose. There were differences among the rebuilds; for example, 488 initially retained its steam-heat equipment.

The FL9s outlived all of Amtrak's other E and F units by several years because of their unusual dual-mode capabilities. The FL9 fleet was overhauled again between 1990 and 1993, this time at Amtrak's Beech Grove shops. Among other changes, the 16-567 engines were replaced with more modern 16-645E versions. From the late 1970s until the mid-1990s, when they were gradually supplanted by new Genesis 2 dual-mode units, the six FL9s were standard power on locomotive-hauled Empire Service trains between Albany-Rensselaer and New York. In April 1991, Amtrak shifted Empire Service operations from the traditional NYC routing to Grand Central Terminal to a modified route running via Spuyten Duyvil in the Bronx, down a portion of the old West Side freight line to a purpose-built connector to reach Penn Station. This change resulted in FL9s regularly operating to Penn Station for the first time in decades.

After retirement, Amtrak sold its classic FL9s to tourist train operators, where they were prized for their classic appearance.

486
486
Amtrak

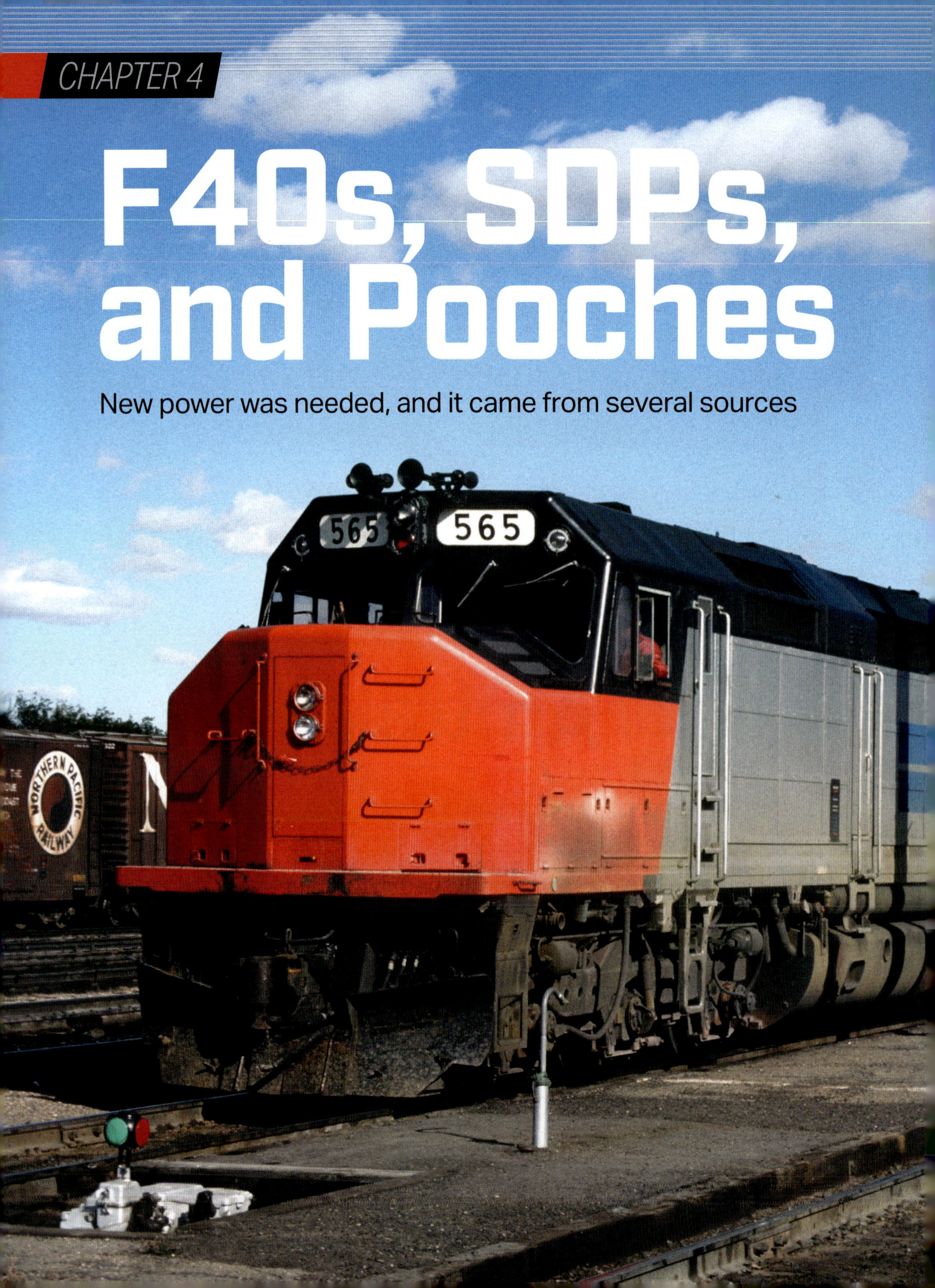

CHAPTER 4

F40s, SDPs, and Pooches

New power was needed, and it came from several sources

For a few years EMD's SDP40Fs were standard power for many long-distance trains. In September 1975, SDP40F 561, with train No. 7, the westbound *Empire Builder,* was photographed on Burlington Northern rails at Havre, Mont. Stability problems at speed doomed the big six-axle diesels, and their service time was short. Most were off the roster by 1981. *George W. Kowanski*

Even in its first days, Amtrak brass recognized the need for new motive power. However, Amtrak was faced with a lack of available purpose-built passenger locomotives from the two primary domestic locomotive suppliers. In the 1960s, the few orders for passenger power had been filled by EMD and GE adapting standard freight designs for passenger service. Amtrak needed modern locomotives with more power than its aging E units, with a design that would work in all terrains and types of service.

It took a couple of tries to get it right, as EMD's short-lived SDP40F (introduced in 1973) and GE's slightly more successful P30CH (1974) gave way to the EMD F40PH, which from its development in 1976 became the face of most non-Northeast Corridor Amtrak trains for the better part of the next two decades. The development, operation, and history of these locomotive groups makes for an interesting story.

The EMD F40PH, originally intended for specialized short- to medium-haul service, became Amtrak's primary long-distance locomotive after problems sidelined the SDP40Fs. On October 12, 1992, F40PHs 379 and 297 led the westbound *Empire Builder* through fall colors in late-afternoon sunlight at Pewaukee, Wis., on Soo Line's former Milwaukee Road main line. *Jeff Wilson*

This publicity photo shows brand-new GE P30CH 714 leading a four-car Amfleet consist on the daylight *Shenandoah,* a train that ran over the Baltimore & Ohio between Washington, D.C., and Cincinnati. The P30CHs, GE's answer to heavy passenger locomotives, were equipped with head-end power (HEP) instead of traditional steam generators for car heating and lighting. *Amtrak*

EMD SDP40F: Nos. 500-649

Amtrak's first order for new diesels, placed in November 1972, was to EMD for 40 SDP40Fs, a new six-motor model adapted from the successful SD40-2 freight design. This 3,000-hp model featured the same successful combination of the proven 16-cylinder 645E3 diesel engine and electrical equipment used by the SD40-2, but encased in a sheet-metal cowl, similar to Santa Fe's FP45 that was adapted from the SD45 in 1968. The SDP40F was 72'-4" long (3'-6" inches longer than a standard SD40-2). They weighed 396,000 pounds and rode on HT-C six-axle trucks (all axles powered) geared for 103 mph.

At that time Amtrak cars still relied on steam heat, so the SDP40F was equipped with a pair of Vapor OK-4625 steam generators. Since the locomotive was intended for cross-country long-distance service, it required a significant volume of water that was stored in both divided below-frame tanks and supplemental circular tanks located above the frame (in the body ahead of the steam generators; 3,500-gallon total capacity). Amtrak anticipated the eventual conversion of its passenger car fleet to electric head-end power (HEP), and some SDP40Fs were built with the provision to add HEP equipment, although none of these locomotives lasted long enough to be converted.

In June 1973, the first SDP40F entered service at Chicago Union Station, just a few miles from EMD's La Grange, Ill., plant. Early SDP40F assignments included the Chicago-Los Angeles *Super Chief.* Amtrak soon

New EMD SDP40Fs work train No. 8, the eastbound *Empire Builder* from Seattle, on the Milwaukee Road crossing of the Chicago & North Western at Mayfair in Chicago on July 29, 1975. *Mike Abalos*

ordered another 110 units, with deliveries starting in late 1973; the fleet was allocated road numbers 500 to 649. In most respects the two orders of SDP40Fs were similar, but there were some differences. The first 40 units had a slightly pointed nose section, and more closely resembled Santa Fe's FP45s and other early cowl models. The later SDP40Fs locomotives had a flat center nose section.

Many SDP40Fs were delivered in Amtrak's first standard paint scheme (classified as Phase I), with platinum mist bodies, large Arrow logos consisting of Amtrak Heritage Blue and Amtrak Red bands on the sides, with red nose sections and black roofs and underbodies. Later locomotives were painted in the Phase II livery, featuring large red and blue wraparound stripes running the length of the body.

The new diesels were impressive looking, and were significantly more powerful and reliable than most of the high-mileage heritage locomotives. However, soon after the SDPs entered service, crew members reported that the new locomotives exhibited excessive lateral sway at high speeds. In their first few years of operation, SDP40Fs were involved in 17 derailments. Extensive

"Soon after the SDP40Fs entered service, crew members reported that the new locomotives exhibited excessive lateral sway at high speeds."

testing was conducted to find the cause, and while tests proved inconclusive, a prevailing opinion was that water tanks with a high center of gravity, combined with the three-axle, three-motor, hollow-bolster HT-C trucks, may have contributed to derailments.

Several host railroads banned the model or imposed serious speed restrictions on the SDP40F, and the National Transportation Safety Board recommended that several of Amtrak's modern six axle locomotives face speed restrictions in curves. This significantly hampered scheduling and operations, and Amtrak was under pressure from host railroads to find a solution.

By the time the SDP40F controversies were getting serious, Amtrak had received the F40PHs, the more compact four-axle locomotive that offered several significant advantages (see page 94). The F40PH tracked well and was equipped with HEP. Amtrak's decision to adopt HEP on a wide scale, combined with the SDP40F's problems, led the railroad to abandon the SDP40F model just a few years after adopting it. Amtrak worked with EMD to trade in most of its SDP40Fs for credit on new F40PHs, and in many instances components from

535
535

Here's a fireman's view of a meet between *Empire Builders* near Chicago's A2 tower in October, 1974. The view from the cab of an SDP40F on the westbound train (Amtrak No. 7) looks toward its eastward counterpart. A Chicago & North Western commuter train is on the right. *Jim Hediger*

Against the backdrop of the famous Gateway Arch in St. Louis, SDP40Fs 597 and 591 power the westbound *National Limited* on the eastern approach to the MacArthur Bridge over the Mississippi River. This was a short-lived chapter for Amtrak; just a few years after this January 1975 photo was exposed, both the *National Limited* and the SDP40Fs were history.
Clyde L. Anderson

SDP40Fs were recycled and rebuilt.

A few SDP40Fs remained in long-distance service until 1982, when Amtrak finally phased out the last of its steam-heated passenger cars. The locomotive newsmagazine *Extra 2200 South* reported that the last regular revenue steam-heated long-distance train was the northbound *Silver Star* of March 9, 1982, led by SDP40Fs 634 and 639. Ironically, the SDP40F fleet barely outlasted the E units they were bought to replace. While the last nine SDP40Fs were turned back to EMD in 1987, not all of the SDP40Fs met this fate. In 1984, Amtrak swapped 18 of them to Santa Fe for 25 CF7 road switchers (see Chapter 6) and SSB1200 switchers. Santa Fe modified the former Amtrak units for freight service, becoming Nos. 5932-5949.

Among the Santa Fe engines that lasted to the BNSF merger was former Amtrak 644. For a promotion it was

painted in a distinctive blue, white, and black scheme and lettered for shipping company Maersk. It was preserved and for several years and displayed at Ogden, Utah, before being moved to the Nevada State Railroad Museum in Boulder City, Nev., where it was displayed as 6976 along with retired Amtrak F40PH 231.

GE P30CH: Nos. 700-724

General Electric's equivalent to EMD's SDP40F was the 3,000-hp, cowl-body P30CH with a boxy cab profile. The locomotive was adapted from GE's common six-axle U30C freight diesel. Amtrak purchased 25 units and was the lone buyer for this specialized model. It was Amtrak's first diesel-electric equipped with head-end power (HEP) and was intended to work with the new HEP-equipped Amfleet I cars.

Delivered in 1974 and numbered 700-724, the P30CHs cost $480,000 per

Below-freezing temperatures on January 29, 1978, exemplify the steam-heat era when many locomotives carried steam generators to supply passenger cars with heat. Note the wisps of steam escaping from SDP40F 518 and passenger cars at 21st Street in Chicago.
Mike Abalos

The era of the SDP40F lasted just a few years. Most of these ill-fated diesel-electrics were traded back to EMD for credit on new F40PHs. Some components were reused (some F40s were designated as F40PHR to indicate that some SDP40F components were incorporated); the remainder of the locomotive was scrapped. Here the nose section of retired Amtrak No. 536 is seen at Pielet Brothers scrapyard in Chicago in May 1981. *Mike Abalos*

unit. They measured 72'-4" long, weighed 386,000 pounds, and were powered by GE's 16-cylinder 7FDL engine. A compartment at the rear of the body housed twin auxiliary diesel engine/generator sets for HEP. They acquired the nickname "Pooches" based on their model designation.

The high-profile SDP40F derailments, as well as incidents with GE's E60 electric locomotives, resulted in speed restrictions being imposed on P30CHs as well. These speed limitations, combined with the comparatively small size of the fleet, led to specialized assignments for P30CHs in their later years.

In 1983, Amtrak assumed operation of the *Auto Train* (Lorton, Va.-Sanford, Fla.) and from the beginning the P30CHs were synonymous with this unique train. *Auto Train* was the heaviest passenger train in North America, and its long strings of auto racks as well as passenger cars could warrant up to four P30CHs to maintain its scheduled speed. Some P30CHs were based out of New Orleans, where they were routinely assigned to the *Sunset Limited*.

The P30CHs were GE orphans in a largely EMD fleet. Their numbers began declining in the mid-1980s, although a few survived into the early 1990s. The lease of a fleet of Helm GP40s in 1991 permitted the last P30CHs to be retired. Ironically, this occurred in December 1991, just as Amtrak was receiving its next significant order for GE diesels in the form of the 500-series Dash 8-32BWHs. All the P30CHs were scrapped.

The first P30CH poses for its builder's portrait at Erie, Pa., in 1975 (top). General Electric built 25 of these locomotives for Amtrak between August and December of that year. The type was the latest passenger adaptation of its six-axle U30C freight diesel, similar in design to the U30CGs built for Santa Fe in 1967. The drawing (above) shows the proposed P30CH prior to construction. The rendering looks more like one of Santa Fe's U30CG cowl diesels than the resulting prototype. *Two images: General Electric*

A transitional lashup of diesels, including Southern Railway E8A 6907A, lead train No. 59, the *City of New Orleans,* at 21st Street in Chicago on March 21, 1979. General Electric P30CH 712 is in the lead, with EMD F40PH 265 ahead of the baggage car. *Mike Abalos*

EMD F40PH: Nos. 200–415

To many transportation observers, the F40PH was "the diesel that saved Amtrak." From its introduction in 1976, the 3,000-hp, four-axle diesel emerged as the dominant long-distance passenger locomotive. The F40PH proved to be a powerful, adaptable, durable locomotive that carried Amtrak through decades of funding challenges beset with political complications. Its design proved itself again and again over the years, and it was widely purchased by commuter agencies and other passenger operators. It served as the face of Amtrak for a generation of train riders until gradually supplanted by Genesis models in the 1990s and early 2000s.

Amtrak's early plans for new diesels were for the six-axle, six-motor locomotives to lead long-haul service with the four-motor F40PH leading Corridor trains with the new Amfleet cars. However, when problems developed with the SDP40F, Amtrak shifted its focus to the F40PH, which emerged as the standard workhorse diesel.

As mentioned earlier, the specialized nature of passenger locomotives, combined with their comparatively small (and uncertain) sales potential, meant major American locomotive builders lowered costs by adapting existing freight locomotive designs to passenger applications. This philosophy yielded mixed results with some commuter rail models and Amtrak's SDP40F and P30CH diesels (as well as GE E60 electrics), which proved to be less than ideal locomotives. The F40PH, however, proved to be the exception.

Electro-Motive created the F40PH for Amtrak by starting with its successful GP40-2 freight locomotive, adding a cowl covering, and making electrical changes to provide HEP power. It used EMD's highly successful 16-cylinder 645E3 diesel and AR10-D14 alternator. It measured 56'-2" long, and Amtrak's designated standard weight was 262,000 pounds. Most of Amtrak's F40PH fleet employed a 57:20 gear ratio for a top speed of 103 mph; Nos. 329 to 360 had a 56:21 gear ratio for a 110-mph top speed. The listed cost of the first F40PH (number 200) was $538,735 in 1976, but by 1988, a new F40PH was estimated at more than $1.3 million.

A significant innovation was the F40PH's HEP generation system, which used the main 645 diesel to power the auxiliary HEP generator. This arrangement altered the traditional operation of the locomotive and the role of the throttle. On most diesel electrics the throttle has eight running positions that match engine output to speed demands. On an F40PH, the engineer can set the auxiliary HEP generator to one of three operating positions: normal, standby, and isolate. These settings alter the speed of the diesel engine for HEP requirements rather than traction demands.

In the "normal" position, the 645 engine operates continually at maximum speed (893 rpm), and as a result, F40PHs roar even when standing still. The "standby" position reduces engine speed to 720 rpm — still significantly faster than normal 645 idling speed. So, in situations when engine speed was governed by HEP demands, the engineer's throttle controls excitation of the main generator to modulate the current supplied to traction motors, rather than its conventional function of matching the engine and generator output.

In the "isolate" position, no HEP is being produced, so the locomotive operates as a normal diesel-electric, with

The P30CH, built solely for Amtrak, used a pair of 12V715 Detroit Diesels and electrical equipment to generate head-end power (HEP). This gear was located in compartments at the rear of the locomotive, marked by grills on either side of the rear-end door. On March 30, 1980, head-end crews confer during a station stop at the depot in downtown Houston, Texas, at the front of P30CH 717 on the *Inter-American*.
Tom Kline

Top: A crew change for the Portland-Chicago *Pioneer,* train No. 26, takes place on Union Pacific at Hinkle, Ore., on September 5, 1978. Amtrak's first series of F40PHs (200-229) had less fuel and HEP capacity than its later F40s and so only rarely worked western long distance trains after the Superliners became standard equipment. *J. David Ingles*

Above: Amtrak F40PH 259 leads train No. 304, the eastbound *Ann Rutledge,* at Kirk Junction (Kirkwood, Mo.), on November 28, 1986. No. 259 was one of the locomotives sometimes designated "F40PHR," which were ordered in trade for SDP40Fs and reused some components. It wears the broad-stripe Phase II paint that was typical of the original scheme applied to the first F40s. *Scott Muskopf*

the engine speed matching the throttle setting required for traction.

Amtrak received 210 F40PHs from EMD over an 11-year span between 1976 and 1987, 200-409. In addition, it also acquired an additional group of six former GO Transit (Toronto commuter service) F40s in the late 1980s, which were numbered 410-415. The 200 series, previously occupied by E8s, was reassigned to the F40PHs. This honored the American Bicentennial

year when the first locomotives of the fleet were delivered in Amtrak's new patriotic Phase II paint scheme.

The success of the F40PH and the deteriorating situation regarding the SDP40F led Amtrak to trade many of the relatively new SDPs back to EMD as credit for new F40PHs. Locomotives involved in these trade-ins often re-used components; some literature designates these as model F40PHR, but it's not widely used. Recycled components included the engine (16-645E3 diesel), traction motors, and cooling fans.

Amtrak performed major overhauls on F40PHs about every 750,000 miles of service (roughly about every 6 years), but by the 1990s the locomotives were showing their age. Many had been rebuilt two or more times, and some had passed 2 million miles of service. This spurred Amtrak in 1993 and 1994 to conduct a detailed analysis of the F40PH fleet, with the goal to improve

Making smoke as they take a gentle curve east of Dayton, Texas, P30CH 719 and a sister unit lead train No. 2, the *Sunset Limited,* toward New Orleans on August 22, 1986. *Tom Kline*

the locomotives' reliability by at least 25 percent. A team reviewed and carefully examined component failure data for each of the 10 series of engines and compared data with information conducted from physical examinations of the 199 surviving active F40PHs at that time. The oldest locomotives, along with the secondhand GO Transit units, were experiencing the most problems.

The study considered the advantages of completely remanufacturing the F40 fleet. This would have included replacing the existing engines with modern 12-cylinder 710G3B diesels, installing state-of-the-art traction motors, and installing an advanced EMD EM-2000 microprocessor-controlled electrical system. Had this option been exercised, the estimated price tag was about $1.2 million per locomotive (about half the price of a brand-new Genesis locomotive), but would have resulted in essentially new locomotives with up to 15 years of additional service life.

However, with new Genesis locomotives already being delivered, Amtrak instead chose to continue overhauling the F40s in-kind at its Beech Grove Shops, while implementing minor changes: addition of ditch lights, installing recessed cab-entry steps, adding improved radiator and dynamic brake hatches, and doing body work and painting as needed.

The F40PHs were gradually phased out with arrival of additional Genesis and F59PHI locomotives. By 1995, Amtrak had a surplus of F40PHs, in part owing to deliveries of new locomotives but also as result of budget cuts that had reduced service levels. Twenty F40s were leased to Union Pacific for freight service, and Amtrak opted to convert

On May 9, 1993, F40PH 321 works train No. 477 (the westbound *Bay State*) along the Quaboag River at West Warren, Mass., leading three Amfleet cars. For about a dozen years from the mid-1980s through the mid-1990s, Amtrak operated so-called Inland Corridor trains over Conrail's Boston Line between Boston and Springfield, Mass., which then continued via Hartford and New Haven to New York and Washington, D.C. *Jeff Wilson*

some F40PHs into engineless cab-control and cab/baggage cars, designated as "non-powered control units" (NPCUs). These came to known colloquially as "cabbages" (see Chapter 7). Completion of Northeast Corridor electrification to Boston further eliminated the need for the older road diesels.

Among the last regular assignments for the venerable locomotives was in the Northeast, working Springfield, Mass.,-New Haven, Conn., shuttles, the Washington-St. Albans, Vt., *Vermonter*, and the New York-Toronto *Maple Leaf*. By the end of 2003 most F40s were off the roster, however many found new homes with other rail operators.

GMD GP40TC/GP38H-3: Nos. 192-199 (520-527)

In autumn 1966, GO Transit — the Government of Ontario's Toronto-area suburban-service operator — took delivery of eight GP40TC diesels, a specialized model built by EMD's Canadian affiliate, General Motors Diesel. This was a pioneering commercially produced diesel designed to deliver head-

The southbound *Texas Eagle* pauses at the Santa Fe depot in McGregor, Texas, on August 24, 1992. Two charter busloads (left) of passengers are boarding at the brick platform in this small Texas town. Only one F40PH was needed to haul the seven-car train, which will terminate at San Antonio; some of its cars will be added to the *Sunset Limited*. *Tom Kline*

Amtrak F40PH 404 rolls west with a matched consist of five Horizon cars on a *San Joaquin* bound for Oakland in November 1990. The train is passing the C&H sugar processing plant at Crockett, Calif. The 404 is from the final order of F40PHs, delivered in 1988. *Brian Solomon*

The Toronto-bound *Maple Leaf* races westward near Corfu, N.Y., where on May 10, 1892, New York Central & Hudson River 4-4-0 No. 999 made its world-famous speed run. The *Maple Leaf* was among the last regular runs for Amtrak's F40PH diesels. Locomotive 301 displays late-life modifications stemming from its mid-1990s overhaul, including front-facing ditch lights. *Brian Solomon*

end power (HEP) to all-electric commuter cars.

It was a novel adaptation of EMD's recently introduced 3,000-hp GP40 freight model, powered by the new turbocharged 16-645E3 diesel engine. Although a four-axle locomotive, the GP40TC used the longer SD40 frame and featured an abnormally long rear hood to accommodate the auxiliary 12-cylinder diesel and 600kW alternator for HEP (a typical GP40 measured 59'-2", while the GP40TC was 65'-7"). In 1988, after more than two decades of service in Canada, Amtrak purchased the entire fleet and initially assigned them to passenger service numbered 192-199, sequentially preceding the

In September 2000, Amtrak's former New Haven Shore Line route was undergoing a major transformation. After years of discussion, the line had been electrified and significant portions of track were upgraded for speeds up to 150 mph in preparation of Acela Express high speed service. However, some trains were still being hauled by two-decade-old F40PH diesels, as with westbound 278 at Stonington, Conn.
Brian Solomon

F40PH fleet. Some Amtrak sources classified the units as GP40H, other sources have used the GP40PH designation.

In the mid-1990s, Amtrak renumbered them 520-527 to make room for new GE P42s that were numbered 1-207. In 2004 and 2005, the locomotives were rebuilt at Norfolk Southern's Juniata Shops at Altoona, Pa. Work included replacing the turbocharger with a blower (derating output to 2,000 hp), upgrading electronics, and reclassifying them as GP38H-3. They retained head-

end power and their 520-series numbers. Since rebuilding, they have served in work train service and are used as standby road locomotives for rescue service.

They are among the older EMD's painted in a minimalistic variation of the Phase V scheme with the majority of the body dressed in plain Platinum Mist, with Amtrak Blue on the top and Anthracite Gray for the underbody, trucks, walkways, steps, and top of the short hood (to minimize reflection). They carry Amtrak's Travelmark logo on their cab sides with large road numbers on each hood side below the radiator intakes.

GP40s: 650-664

In the early 1990s, Amtrak leased a fleet of 15 GP40s from Helm as a temporary measure to overcome a motive power shortage before the first Genesis P40 diesels were delivered. These were regeared to a 57:20 ratio to make them compatible with F40s and allow operation at normal passenger train speeds.

These GP40s were not HEP-equipped, but they received pass-through HEP cables to allow head-end power from leading units to reach passenger cars. Numbered 650-664, these were honorary B-units, as they typically operated in trailing positions in consists led by F40PHs.

↑ Train No. 318, the *Hoosier State*, pauses in the street on CSX's former Monon at Lafayette, Ind., to make its nocturnal station stop en route from Chicago to Indianapolis. On March 8, 1992, the train is led by Amtrak No. 192, a former GO Transit GP40TC. *Scott Muskopf*

← Amtrak's former GO Transit GP40TCs were rebuilt by Norfolk Southern in Juniata, Pa., in 2004 and 2005. They were reclassified as GP38H-3 (520-527) and largely reassigned to work train service and train-rescue duties. On October 22, 2013, GP38H-3s 522 and 526 cross the Millers River on New England Central's line at Millers Falls, Mass., on their way north to collect a ballast train at Vernon, Vt. *Brian Solomon*

CHAPTER 5

For more than 20 years, General Electric P42 Genesis diesels were the standard road power for most Amtrak long distance services, assuming the role from the well-regarded EMD F40PH. A pair of P42s in Amtrak's Phase V paint scheme lead the eastbound *Lake Shore Limited* near Palmer, Mass., on June 16, 2012. *Brian Solomon*

Modern diesel fleet

Purpose-built passenger locomotives re-emerged in the 1990s

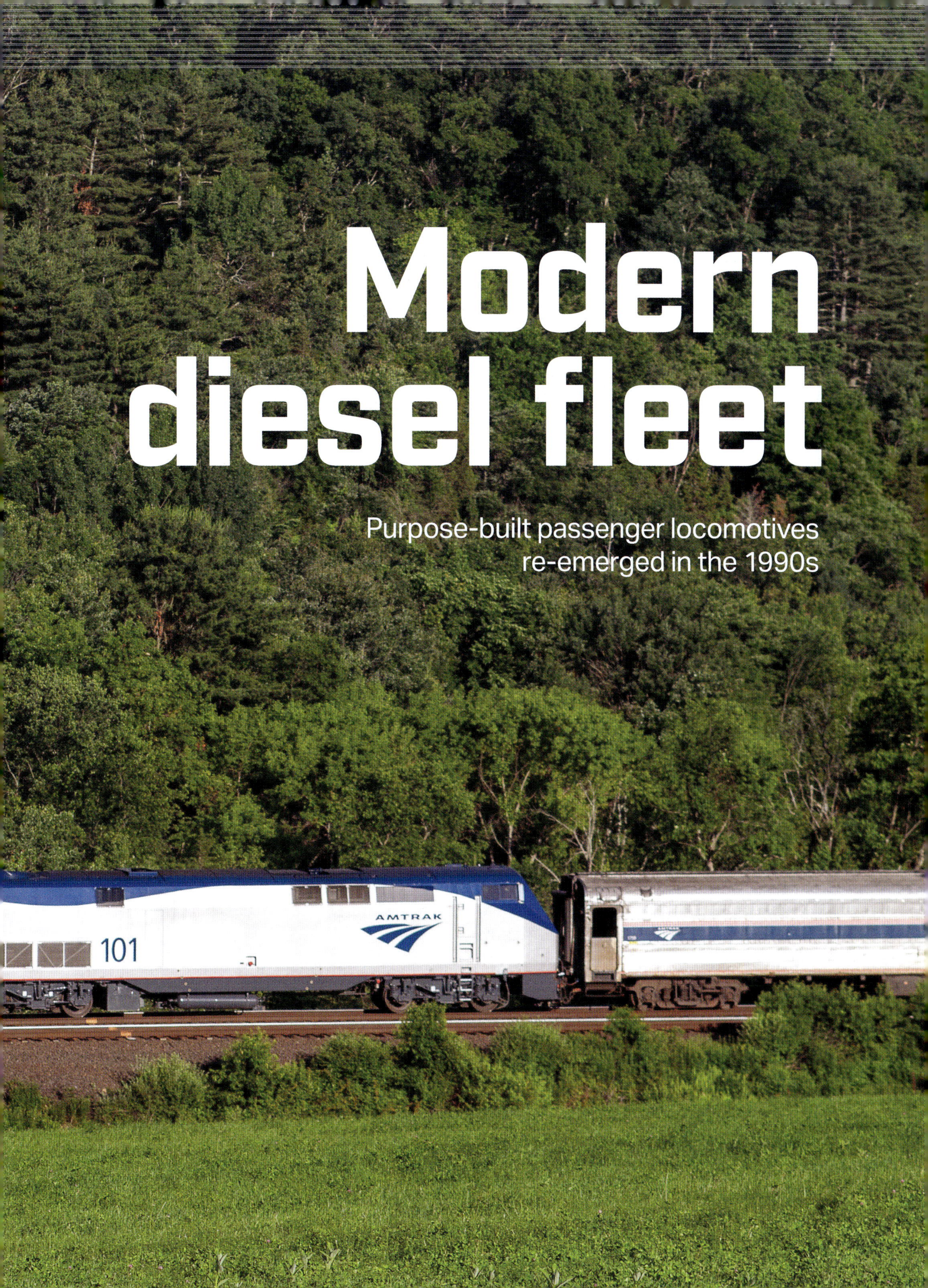

Brand-new GE P32BH 506 arrives in Chicago at the head of train No. 49, the westbound *Lake Shore Limited,* on December 18, 1991. It, along with fellow GE 507 and a pair of F40PHs, is wyeing its train at Canal Street. *Mike Abalos*

With the F40PH, Amtrak hit on a diesel that served its needs well for the better part of two decades. It was, however, still a freight locomotive in passenger sheathing, and by the late 1980s the design was technologically lagging behind new diesels of the period. As the F40s aged, Amtrak again looked for new solution. This time, after a brief stopgap in a modified freight road switcher, it would find a solution in a purpose-built passenger engine, the Genesis series of monocoque-body locomotives.

As the F40 did in the 1970s, the General Electric-built Genesis locomotives would become the standard for Amtrak long-distance trains from the 1990s onward. They would hold the title until another purpose-built locomotive, the Siemens Mobility Charger, appeared in the 2020s. These locomotives, featuring new streamlined bodies, specially designed high-speed trucks, microprocessor control, and many other internal upgrades and innovations, would not be misidentified from freight locomotives.

As built, Amtrak's 20 General Electric Dash 8-32BWH diesels — designated P32BH by Amtrak — featured a distinctive paint scheme that earned them the moniker "Pepsi Cans." In May 1997, No. 519, the highest-numbered in the series, paused at Carbondale, Ill., for a station stop and crew change.
Scott Muskopf

GE P32BH: Nos. 500-519

But first, we need to take a short side trip. In 1991, Amtrak took a different direction with its motive power acquisition by placing an order with General Electric for the first time since the early 1970s. This was initially for 52 new diesels, with the first subgroup of 20 units adapted from GE's Dash 8 freight diesels and the larger part for newly designed locomotives built to the AMD-103 specification (leading to the Genesis design — see page 110).

General Electric designated the first group as Dash 8-32BWH: Dash 8 line, 3,200 hp, B (two-axle trucks), Wide nose, Head-end-power equipped. Amtrak's designation of P32BH followed GE's earlier model designation formula and is used throughout this book.

The P32BH was the first application of GE's Dash 8 technology for Amtrak service. The Dash 8 line had been refined in the mid-1980s for high-horsepower freight locomotives, and greatly contributed to GE surpassing EMD as America's leading diesel-electric manufacturer. Innovations included onboard microprocessor controls to optimize engine performance, improve fuel efficiency, control wheel slip, and ensure greater reliability. It was employed to improve locomotive performance in a specific application without requiring substantial changes to mechanical or electrical components.

General Electric patterned Amtrak's units on its high-horsepower Dash 8-40BW, which it had developed a year earlier for Santa Fe's high-priority "Super Fleet" transcontinental intermodal service. These were among GE's first locomotives to incorporate the new North American Safety Cab, and noteworthy for their good fuel economy and exceptional reliability. Like Santa Fe's new engines, Amtrak's P32BHs were numbered in the 500 block (previously occupied by SDP40Fs). The two GE models shared external dimensions, and had a very similar appearance. However, where the freight locomotive

In August 1992, 501 — one of two P32BHs bought by Caltrans — leads a state-sponsored *Capitol* train on Southern Pacific street trackage at Jack London Square in Oakland. *Brian Solomon*

General Electric P32BH 505 wears the short-lived Phase IV livery. It is seen at the back of a push-pull set of California Cars serving a Sacramento-bound *Capitol* at Davis, Calif., on November 9, 2003. *Brian Solomon*

was powered by GE's 16-cylinder FDL engine to deliver 4,000 hp for traction, Amtrak's 500 series GEs employed a 12-cylinder FDL that produced 3,200 hp for traction and also powered an auxiliary alternator for head-end power (HEP).

Amtrak debuted a stylish new paint scheme on these locomotives, the design and colors of which led to the locomotives' unofficial moniker as "Pepsi Cans." The first of the fleet, 500, was

Amtrak P32BH 509, wearing the Phase IV scheme, leads the *Lake Country Limited* west of Long Lake, Ill., on March 22, 2001, two days before the short-lived Chicago-Janesville, Wis., service was reduced to Saturday-only operation. On this day the train consisted of a Horizon coach, a heritage baggage car, private car *St. James Place,* and five RoadRailers carrying express freight. *Chris Guss*

tested by GE at its Erie, Pa., plant in September 1991. Engine 501, the first delivered to Amtrak (in November), was sent to Washington D.C., for a dedication ceremony. The bulk of the order was delivered that December.

Initially, the P32BHs were based in Los Angeles and were largely assigned to trains serving California. Numbers 501 and 502 were financed by Caltrans and carried state markings as well as Amtrak lettering. These were routinely assigned to California's sponsored trains, including the *San Joaquin* (Oakland-Bakersfield), and *Capitols* (San Jose-Sacramento). The rest of the fleet typically worked long-distance trains including the *California Zephyr* (Chicago-Oakland), *Coast Starlight* (Los Angeles-Seattle), *Desert Wind* (Chicago-Los Angeles via Salt Lake City), *Southwest Chief* (Chicago-Los Angeles via Kansas City), and *Sunset Limited* (Los Angeles-New Orleans).

After the delivery of Genesis P42 units, some P32BHs were reassigned to Midwestern corridor trains and as switchers around the system. Some were repainted in a variation of the Phase IV livery and most ended up dressed in a minimal variation of the Phase V scheme. Caltrans retained its pair of engines (renumbered 2051 and 2052), which were repainted in a variation of the Amtrak California livery. As of 2024, most P32BHs remained active.

GE Genesis

In the 1970s and 1980s, Amtrak had purchased passenger adaptations of common freight locomotives with mixed results. By far the most success-

On November 9, 2013, a *Hiawatha* train departs Milwaukee behind P32-8 506. Although the P32BH's heyday as premium power for long-distance trains was short-lived, this small fleet of GE diesels has had a long and productive career spanning more than three decades.
Brian Solomon

ful was EMD's F40PH, but by the early 1990s they were aging and Amtrak was anticipating the need to invest in a significant fleet of more-modern locomotives. Rather than rely on further adaptation of existing types, Amtrak innovated.

Amtrak aimed to incorporate European technological advancements into state-of-the-art, lightweight, purpose-built passenger locomotives that, with light axle weight and compact clearances, could operate on all of its routes across the continent without restriction. Amtrak's AMD-103 specifications stood for Amtrak Diesel, 103-mph maximum speed (although some sources say "AMD" was for Amtrak Monocoque Diesel). Amtrak issued the specifications, and GE and EMD were encouraged to offer competitive bids.

In 1991, GE presented the winning bid, securing a large order for new diesels that included the 20 P32-BWH locomotives described earlier, and collaborated with Amtrak for a modern diesel based on the AMD-103 specs. General Electric held a contest among its employees to name the new locomotive type, and the winning name was Genesis — a name which cleverly blends the manufacturers' initials with the concept of "coming into being" that conveyed a whole new generation of locomotives.

Not since the late-1950s had GE been involved in an effort to create a new diesel-electric type specifically tailored for the demands of American passenger service. Except for MLW's LRC locomotives, the prior four decades of North American diesel devel-

⬆ Key to the design of the Genesis units was the monocoque body, which provides strength and allows a low center of gravity. The locomotive's low profile was designed to present minimal clearance issues, allowing it to be used on virtually any route. It's narrower and shorter than typical North American freight locomotives, which is clearly evident in this July 22, 2010, comparison of P40 110 working the *Vermonter* alongside CSX GP40-2 6237 on local freight B740 at Palmer, Mass. *Brian Solomon*

Amtrak industrial designer César Vergara is credited for the innovative Genesis body style as well as its original paint scheme, which featured fading stripes toward the back of the locomotive. A pair of P40s work back-to-back on train No. 4, the eastbound *Southwest Chief,* near Ancona, Ill., on March 25, 1995. *Brian Solomon*

opment had been focused on refining heavy freight locomotives. Passenger locomotives, when needed, had been merely adapted from freight designs. What emerged with the Genesis collaboration was fundamentally, completely different than any existing American diesels.

The design incorporated two innovations from German manufacturer Krupp. In place of the standard North American practice of basing the locomotive on a heavy, fabricated frame riding on cast trucks, the Genesis employed a Krupp-built integral monocoque body shell riding on fabricated trucks of its design. Krupp supplied the first 11 body shells with the remainder constructed by GE. The monocoque shell — like a cylindrical tube — offers a high strength-to-weight ratio, eliminating the need for a heavy frame.

The modern fabricated trucks are a bolsterless flexicoil design with hydraulic shock absorbers and lateral yaw dampers, and they were free from sliding surfaces. The trucks were specifically designed for stability at high speeds

On November 6, 2021, P42 108 — painted to mark Amtrak's 50 years of service — leads train No. 42, the eastbound *Pennsylvanian,* through Christiana, Pa., under catenary on the former Pennsylvania Railroad main line. *Patrick Yough*

EMD'S EXPERIMENTAL F69PHAC

Electro-Motive built a pair of F69PHAC diesels in 1989 as experimental models. They served as a test bed for applying recently developed European three-phase AC traction to North American locomotives. This was a significant application of Siemens AG's AC traction system that had been developed in Germany.

Two locomotives (450 and 451) were built in 1989, lettered for Amtrak, and initially dressed in the common Phase III paint scheme that was typical of contemporary F40PHs. They featured an unusual cab arrangement similar to that applied to F40PHM-2s built for Chicago's Metra around the same time. On these, the sloped front windows connected directly with the top front of the locomotive nose without the cab-window/nose section inset typical of the F40PH and other contemporary EMD passenger diesels.

Unit 450 was initially owned by Amtrak, while EMD retained ownership of 451. The two units entered service in 1990 and initially operated together on test runs. Both were powered by EMD's 12-cylinder 710G3 engine and employed an alternator with rectifiers that supplied DC to twin banks of Freon-cooled static inverters. The inverters in turn converted the DC to polyphase AC (480V at 60Hz) to power four AC traction motors (one on each axle), connected in parallel. Each inverter supplied power to two motors.

In 1993, both F69PHACs were repainted to match the Siemens ICE high-speed trainset imported from Germany, and were lettered "Amtrak Siemens Electro Motive." They were assigned to haul the ICE train on its demonstration runs outside of electrified territory.

The F69s provided important research data and real-world experience in AC traction for EMD, which eventually resulted in the pioneering SD70MAC freight locomotive, which was America's first mass-produced diesel-electric using modern polyphase AC traction. The F69PHAC itself was not mass-produced — Amtrak didn't place orders for EMD diesels with AC traction, and its fleets of EMD F59PHIs in the 1990s employed conventional DC traction. In 1993, Amtrak sold 450 back to EMD.

Amtrak F69PHAC 450 is testing at 18th Street in Chicago on September 5, 1990. Two of these experimental three-phase, AC-traction diesels worked Amtrak trains in the early 1990s. *Mike Abalos*

The two experimental EMD F69PHAC diesels were repainted to match the German ICE high-speed trainset and lettered for Amtrak, Siemens, and Electro-Motive to lead the imported electric train on its American tour outside of electrified territory. The revolutionary diesels work an eastbound press run at Providence, R.I., on September 14, 1993. *Walter E. Zullig, Jr.*

The eastbound *California Zephyr* catches the glint of the setting sun as it rolls along former Chicago, Burlington & Quincy tracks at Congress Park, Ill., on its final leg toward Chicago Union Station. In the lead is Genesis P42 152 on November 9, 2013. *Brian Solomon*

152
AMTRAK

"The monocoque shell of the Genesis provides a high strength-to-weight ratio, eliminating the need for a heavy frame."

(unlike conventional freight-locomotive trucks), and provided a lightweight, high-tractive-effort, twin-axle arrangement unlike anything else in modern North American service.

To comply with Amtrak's most restrictive mainline clearances, notably in the tunnels serving New York area terminals, required lower and narrower dimensions than typical diesel-electrics — the Genesis locomotives are 14'-6" tall and 10'-0" wide. Amtrak's chief designer, Cèsar Vergara, created a thoroughly modern appearance that avoided complex curves by employing angular construction with flat surfaces. Vergara also developed the original Genesis paint livery, now considered an adaptation of the Phase III scheme, which featured broad stripes that followed the angles of the nose profile while incorporating a fading stripe toward the back of the locomotive. The later version of this scheme as employed on P42DC models feature solid stripes. Amtrak's Genesis caught the attention of the design community and won awards for industrial design including the prestigious Brunel Award. Today, Vergara is one of the most respected names in railroad industrial design with the Genesis being one of his most recognizable achievements.

At the core of Genesis Series 1 locomotives (GE model Dash 8-40BP, des-

⬆ Charging through the junction at Dalies, N.M., a pair of P40s bracketing a P32BH "Pepsi Can" lead the eastbound *Southwest Chief.* The train is diverging from Santa Fe's "Transcon" onto the old main line that will take it via Albuquerque and over Glorieta and Raton Passes and on to Kansas City and ultimately Chicago. *Tom Kline*

⬅ Two-year-old P40 841 sails across the highland prairie near Colmor, N.M., at the lead of train No. 4, the eastbound *Southwest Chief,* on September 26, 1995. *Tom Kline*

A pair of General Electric P40 Genesis Series 1 diesels are on the head end of the *California Zephyr* as it begins its westward journey through the maze of tracks at Chicago Union Station on August 28, 1994. *Brian Solomon*

ignated by Amtrak as the P40) were the latest GE Dash 8-era diesel-electric systems, including its refined 7FDL-16 diesel engine rated at 4,000 hp, a GMG 195A1 alternator, and four DC GE752AH8 traction motors. The 74:29 gear ratio allowed the locomotive to meet the 103-mph design spec. A fully loaded P40 weighs 268,240 pounds and delivers 38,500 pounds of tractive effort at 33 mph. An auxiliary alternator provides three-phase 480VAC for HEP. The P40 has 2,200-gallon fuel tanks.

In addition to its trucks and body, the model set several other significant precedents including pioneer application of an electrically controlled "parking brake" (instead of the old-school mechanical hand brake) and was one of the first locomotives to use modern desktop-style throttle and brake controls in the cab.

The first Genesis locomotives were 44 P40s built by GE at Erie, Pa., between 1993 and 1994 (800-843). The Genesis made its public debut in Amtrak service in June 1993, with locomotives 802 and 804 assigned to the Lorton, Va.-Sanford, Fla., *Auto Train.* The type has led that train's operations ever since, replacing the old GE P30CHs that held the run for years. The P40s are the preferred locomotive in this service because their older 26L air-brake schedules better enables skilled engineers to use a power-braking (stretch-braking) technique to provide a smoother ride with the long, heavy consists typical of *Auto Train.*

The P40s proved less useful to Amtrak on other runs than the much larger fleet of later P42DCs (see page 121) and many P40s were sidelined after just a decade of service. Four were later sold to NJ Transit, and another eight were leased and later sold to the Connecticut Department of Transportation, which later acquired the four NJ Transit units. These have worked a variety of services on Metro-North, Shore Line, and Hartford Line routes.

In 2010 and 2011, Amtrak rebuilt and upgraded more than a dozen P40s to P42DC specifications, and these retained their 800-series numbers.

⬆ Genesis locomotives likely wore more special paint schemes than any other Amtrak diesel. Here P42 189 wears the special Heartland Flyer "Big Game" scheme as it whisks the westbound *Sunset Limited* over the Sunset Route's Terminal Subdivision near West Junction in Houston, Texas, on April 2, 2014. *Tom Kline*

⬅ General Electric built P40 822 in 1993 as part of Amtrak's original order for Genesis diesels. It became one if 15 P40s refurbished, upgraded, and restored to service by the Beech Grove shops as part of the American Recovery and Investment Act of 2009, and was among the locomotives repainted in heritage liveries in 2011 for Amtrak's 40th Anniversary. Here it poses with the Exhibit Train at Springfield, Mass., on July 9, 2011. *Brian Solomon*

P42DC

Ultimately, GE produced three variations of Genesis diesels. All employed the same basic monocoque shell, and while they appear nearly identical externally, there are significant internal differences. For its later Genesis models, GE adopted Amtrak's designation scheme. The most common is the P42DC, a 4,200-hp version that was in production from 1996 until 2001; they are numbered 1-207. The P42DC benefitted from GE's later Dash-9 technology that features a variety of refinements including advanced microprocessor controls and electronic fuel injection to improve locomotive performance. These also have a top speed of 110 mph. In the nearly 30 years since their introduction, the P42s became the most familiar long-distance passenger locomotive assigned to trains across the network. As of 2024, the P42 fleet is gradually being thinned as modern

⬆ September 25, 1997, was a beautiful early autumn day on CSX's former Baltimore & Ohio main line as Train 30, the eastbound *Capitol Limited,* approaches Hyndman, Pa., with pair of new P42 Genesis diesels on the point. High clearances on this route allowed operation of Superliner equipment, which made the *Capitol Limited* one of few Eastern trains to take advantage of the high-capacity bilevel cars. *Brian Solomon*

Siemens Mobility Chargers (see page 134) become more common.

The earliest P42s were delivered in a variation of the Phase III livery, similar to that applied to the 800-series P40s, but without the fade effect on the striping at rear. Some were briefly painted in variations of the Phase IV scheme, but the model is most familiar in the Phase V scheme. This features a prominent Amtrak Blue nose that carries in a wave pattern across the top of the largely Platinum Mist body. Prominent Travelmark logos are displayed on the sides with a large road number at the back, with a gray underbody.

The Genesis models have served as greatly varied rolling canvases; no other type of Amtrak locomotive has seen as many special liveries applied. In 2011, Amtrak painted several P42s and other Genesis models in retro-heritage schemes adapted to represent its earlier standard schemes in commemoration for the railroad's 40th anniversary. In addition, a variety of the locomotives have been painted in several commemorative schemes over the years.

For three decades these have been the standard motive power for Amtrak's Empire Service trains originating from Penn Station, working the former NYC along the Hudson and beyond, but they've rarely worked elsewhere. Commuter rail operator Metro-North followed Amtrak's lead and also bought a fleet of P32AC-DMs for its Grand Central-based commuter trains.

The P32AC-DM is powered by GE's 12-cylinder 7FDL diesel engine, and

← General Electric P42 53 shows off fresh paint at Albany-Rensselaer, N.Y., on February 9, 2002. The P42 diesel in the Phase V scheme was the face of Amtrak for two decades. *Brian Solomon*

↓ General Electric P32AC-DM No. 700 leads an eastbound *Empire* train along the Mohawk River at Lock 10 near Hoffmans, N.Y., on October 30, 1998. These dual-mode locomotives work as diesel-electrics in normal service and can draw current from the electrified third rail in the New York terminal area to serve Penn Station. *Brian Solomon*

P32AC-DM

The dual-service (electric/diesel-electric) P32AC-DM was the second Genesis model. The fleet was delivered in two orders, built in 1995 (700-709) and 1998 (710-717). This specialized model was acquired specifically for Empire Corridor service between Albany-Rensselaer and New York's Penn Station. Designed as the successor to EMD's FL9, the P32AC-DM is a 3,200-hp, AC traction locomotive with ability to gather power from an electric third rail or use its own diesel engine.

Paint schemes were in transition on Amtrak's Genesis P42 diesels in October 2001, as east- and westbound *Capitol Limiteds* meet under the complex web of catenary near K Tower at Washington Union Station. At right, the westbound train features units in the Phase III and phase IV schemes, while at the left the eastbound train displays the new Phase V livery that had just been introduced. *Brian Solomon*

122

This view of P42s 100 and 145 with train No. 449, the westbound Boston section of the *Lake Shore Limited*, offers a good perspective of the tops of Genesis locomotives. Unit 145 was one of several "heritage units" repainted into the Phase III scheme that had typified Amtrak locomotives of the 1980s and 1990s. They're shown here on July 2, 2011. *Brian Solomon*

Train No. 331, a Milwaukee-bound *Hiawatha,* passes Rondout Tower on Canadian Pacific's former Milwaukee Road main line on May 17, 2011. P42 145 was one of several GE units dressed in throwback "heritage" paint schemes for Amtrak's 40th anniversary. It's an adaptation of the Phase I livery introduced in 1972 and originally applied to EMD E, F, and SDP40F diesels. *Chris Guss*

Rear views of Genesis locomotives are uncommon. General Electric P42 42 was painted in this special scheme to honor America's veterans; it was displayed at the North Carolina Transportation Museum during the Streamliners at Spencer event in 2014. Unlike the earlier P40 and P32AC-DM models, the P42s do not have rear controls or an operator's window. *Brian Solomon*

General Electric P32AC-DM 710 leads an eastbound Empire Corridor train at Albany-Rensselaer, N.Y., in 2002. This was one of several of the dual-mode units painted in a variation of the short-lived Phase IV livery that gave the P32AC-DM a distinctive appearance, with the gray extending down the front to the striping. *Brian Solomon*

Norfolk Southern SD60E 6920 and Amtrak 42 were both painted to honor military veterans. Both were displayed in Chicago for the Hiring Our Heroes event at Chicago Union Station in July 2013. The event showcased railroad-related jobs available to veterans and their spouses. *Chris Guss*

when in third-rail territory may use retractable third-rail shoes to draw power (750VDC). Instead of the conventional DC traction system used by other Amtrak GEs, the P32AC-DM employs an adaptation of GE's proprietary three-phase AC traction system originally developed for heavy-haul freight locomotives. The engine powers a GMG 199 alternator to supply electricity to four inverters that create AC current used for both traction and HEP.

EMD F59PHI: Nos. 450-470, 2001-2015

Electro-Motive's model F59PHI was an adaptation for Amtrak of the 1980s-era F59PH commuter rail diesel. It stemmed from Amtrak's expansion of its California-supported services, which gained momentum as the result of a 1990 bond issue to help fund statewide passenger services. California led the way in pushing for locomotives with lower carbon emissions, and the California Department of Transportation (CalTrans) worked with EMD to refine a modern equivalent to the F40PH that met the state's lower emission requirements.

Although mechanically and electrically similar to the F59PH, the new locomotive offered a completely new exterior design. The sleek body was EMD's first truly streamlined diesel

since its last E9s were delivered to Union Pacific in 1964. They presented a notable revision to EMD's previous diesels and offered a contrast to GE's contemporary Genesis design.

Caltrans ordered the first nine F59PHIs in January 1993, at an estimated cost of $2.3 million each, for service on state-sponsored *Capitols* and *San Joaquin* trains. They were delivered in 1994 (2001-2009) and painted in a newly designed scheme for Amtrak California services. The body of the locomotive was Amtrak's standard Platinum Mist with a black band on top. Swaths of navy blue formed a wraparound pattern from the nose over the top of the body and below the sill covering fuel tanks, accented with yellow and orange stripes. A new Amtrak California logo of yellow and orange arrows graced the nose, with large "Amtrak California" lettering on the sides with "California Department of Transportation" sublettering at the back of the body. Caltrans ordered additional units (2010-2015) that were delivered in 2001.

What a beautiful way to travel! EMD F59PHI 464 is ready to lead *Pacific Surfliner* train No. 777 on the former Southern Pacific Coast Line route at Simi Valley, Calif., in August 2016. *Brian Solomon*

Engineer Riley Richmond gives a friendly wave from the cab of P42 172 on the inaugural eastbound run of train No. 1340, the *Borealis* (St. Paul-Chicago), near Watertown, Wis., on May 21, 2024. The locomotive is one of a few P42s dressed in the Phase VII paint scheme. *Chris Guss*

AMTRAK
174
174

458
458
458
Amtrak
Amtrak

The F59PHI measures 58'-2" long and weighs 270,000 pounds. The body's aerodynamic cowl shroud helps reduce wind resistance while providing a sleek, streamlined appearance. A fiberglass curved nose covers steel plates designed for collision safety. Power is provided by a 12-cylinder version of EMD's 710G3 diesel. The "I" is for EMD's isolated WhisperCab, which uses an isolating structure and pads to separate the cab from the rest of the body to minimize vibration and noise.

In 1997, EMD built 21 F59PHIs for Amtrak's West Coast services, 450-470. The order was dressed in two distinctly different liveries representing their intended service. The first 16 were painted in the new Pacific Surfliner brand colors, and they match the scheme on purpose-built bilevel passenger cars: Platinum Mist body (including below the sill and trucks) with Amtrak's deep blue paint (a shade that emulates the color of the Pacific Ocean under clear California skies) in a wraparound pattern accented with narrow white stripes and black bands, and additional white sill stripes. They have Amtrak lettering, but notably missing was an Amtrak logo.

↑ EMD F59PHI 2011 leads a westbound *Capitol* (Sacramento-San Jose) at Davis, Calif., in July 2005. The Caltrans-funded F59PHI diesels (2001-2015) were painted in the Amtrak California scheme to match bilevel California Cars assigned to *Capitols* and *San Joaquin* (Oakland-Bakersfield) services. *Brian Solomon*

← *Pacific Surfliner No.* 777 is led by Amtrak F59PHI 454 at CP Madera between Simi Valley and Moorpark, Calif., on August 2, 2016. These compact streamlined diesels match the profile of the bilevel California Cars. *Brian Solomon*

Carolina Department of Transportation's state-funded *Piedmont* trains. NCDOT's F59PHIs were completed in February 1998, and represent an anomaly for Amtrak's diesel operations in the East, where since the mid-1990s most diesel trains were hauled by Genesis models.

The F59PHI's characteristic streamlined nose, top, is constructed from a fiberglass composite and covers protective steel beams and plates designed to shield the engine crew in a collision. The view also shows the modernized EMD B "Blomberg" truck used on the locomotives. The rear view, above, shows the F59's profile. Number 452 is at Los Angeles Union Station on August 4, 2016.

Two photos: Brian Solomon

The last five units, 466-470, were painted to match new Series VI Talgo sets (see page 135) dressed for the recently developed Amtrak Cascades brand. The scheme was designed by a team, led by Amtrak chief designer César Vergara, including Washington State DOT's Office of Rail and Talgo Engineering.

Piggybacked on Amtrak's final F59PHI order was a pair of units built to the same specifications for the North

Siemens Mobility Charger

Amtrak's acquisition of the innovative Siemens Mobility Charger models is directly related to fundamental changes in the objectives of modern American locomotive design. Historically, diesel-electric innovation aimed to improve locomotive performance and reliability, with varying approaches regarding versatility or specialized applications. Except for some specialized freight designs, diesel-electric locomotive output had reached a functional plateau of 4,000 to 4,400 hp in the mid-1990s, with manufacturers perfecting microprocessor controls and other technology. In the late 1990s, however, growing environmental concerns forced a shift toward lowering diesel engine exhaust emissions as the leading objective in new engine design.

The 1990 Clean Air Act Amendments mandated the Environmental Protection Agency to implement engine exhaust emission standards for previously unregulated non-road mobile machines. This included specific mandates regarding railroad locomotives. By the mid-1990s, it was estimated that unregulated locomotive engines contributed approximately 5% of national nitrogen oxide (NOx) emissions. The EPA drafted detailed rules for the construction, remanufacture, and operation of locomotive engines using a phased (tiered) schedule based on original engine manufacture dates.

These rules were detailed in 1997, including a timeline for the first three tiers of emission standards. EPA Tier 0 rules took effect in 2000 and focused on diesel engines built between 1973 and 2001, specifically mandating exhaust-emission thresholds applied to locomotive engine rebuilding. Tier 1 rules set strict standards for locomotives built between 2002 and 2004, and the implementation of these rules coincided with Amtrak's last significant delivery of new locomotives (GE P42s and EMD F59PHIs by the end of 2001), after which the manufacturers effectively ceased production of those models. Although commuter rail operators worked with other builders — notably MPI, Bombardier, and Alstom — to deliver emissions-compliant modern diesels, for the next 15 years Amtrak continued to rely on its existing diesel fleet.

SC44: Nos. 1400-1408 (WSDOT), 2101-2122 (CalTrans), 4601-4633 (IDOT)

Siemens Mobility, which had established a solid reputation with Amtrak through its ACS64 high-speed electrics (Chapter 7), secured a greater share of the American passenger locomotive market with its Charger line of diesel-electrics. This new model was based on

On wintry but sunny November 23, 2010, at East Olympia, Wash., F59PHI 468 whisks a Talgo Series VI trainset working as Amtrak *Cascades* Train 501 (Seattle-Portland). The classic Northwest-theme livery was designed by César Vergara specifically for the Cascades brand.
Jeffrey T. Schultz

Siemens Charger SC44 4613, owned by Illinois DOT and branded for Amtrak Midwest, leads train No. 390, the *Saluki* (Carbondale-Chicago) on November 18, 2018. It's on Metra's approach to the St. Charles Air Line en route to Union Station. It's one of 33 SC44s ordered by the consortium of Midwestern states sponsoring regional services centered on Chicago. *Chris Guss*

a Siemens locomotive platform that had been widely adapted for European applications. The SC44 (*S*iemens *C*harger, *4,4*00 hp) debuted in 2016. They were purchased by state-funded organizations to work Amtrak Midwest, Amtrak California, and Amtrak Cascades medium-distance services.

A key was that the locomotives meet EPA Tier 4 requirements, which took effect in 2015. To this end, Siemens Mobility chose to power the SC44 using a variation of the Cummins QSK95 engine, a 95-liter, 16-cylinder, four-cycle, Tier 4-compliant diesel built in Seymore, Ind. The QSK95 is a modern high-speed engine (its top speed of 1,800 rpm is almost double the speed of a conventional freight diesel) with significantly reduced emissions compared to older diesel engines. The engine uses a liquid catalyst to achieve

emissions (unlike freight diesels, which use mechanical processes). The locomotive employs a modern three-phase AC traction system, where the engine powers an alternator that supplies current to IGBT converters to allow for individual axle control, with a maximum tractive effort of 65,000 pounds.

The locomotives are assembled at Siemens' Mobility Division plant at Florin in Sacramento, Calif. The loco-

Top: On May 31, 2014, North Carolina DOT F59PH 1869 leads train No. 74, a northbound state-sponsored *Piedmont,* at the Salisbury, N.C., station. Built in 1988, the 1869 is one of a half-dozen former GO Transit F59PH diesels on the state's active roster. In addition, NCDOT also acquired similar locomotives from Los Angeles Metrolink, making it one of only a handful of F59PH operators in North America. The F59 model was adapted by EMD for its F59PHI. *Dan Cupper*

Bottom: In 1998, NCDOT bought a pair of EMD F59PHIs built to Amtrak specifications, numbered 1795 and 1797. Here 1797 leads Amtrak train No. 75, the *Piedmont,* at Salisbury, N.C., on May 30, 2014. This state-sponsored service connects Raleigh and Charlotte. *Brian Solomon*

motive measures 71'-6" long and rides on high-speed trucks with 44"-diameter wheels. The Charger truck design is derived from the firm's ACS64 electric locomotive. Truck frames are integrally welded structures that are bolsterless — they employ a center pin and traction pivot design to provide low carbody connections.

As with other contemporary passenger-locomotive designs, the Charger has a monocoque body. It has a large crew cab, desktop controls, and an innovative anticlimber and nose design to disperse energy and protect the cab interior in the event of collisions. The fuel tank capacity is 1,800 gallons.

The first SC44s was completed in mid-2016 for Illinois Department of Transportation (IDOT), which manages the group of 10 state-sponsored services centered on Chicago. These are funded by Illinois, Indiana, Michigan, Missouri, and Wisconsin, and branded as Amtrak Midwest. The 33 IDOT SC44s carry IDTX reporting marks and are numbered 4601-4633.

Caltrans bought 22 SC44s for service on *Capitol Corridor* and *Pacific Surfliner* trains. Before entering service, the first new locomotive was displayed in mid-April 2017 at the California State Railroad Museum in Sacramento for the California Passenger Rail Summit. Units 2101-2108 are painted for Amtrak California services; 2109-2122 carry Pacific Surfliner branding.

A Siemens Mobility SC44 Charger owned by Caltrans and lettered for Pacific Surfliner service rolls its train to a stop at the Fullerton, Calif., station. It's working train No. 768 bound for San Diego on the former Santa Fe in November 2018. *Brian Solomon*

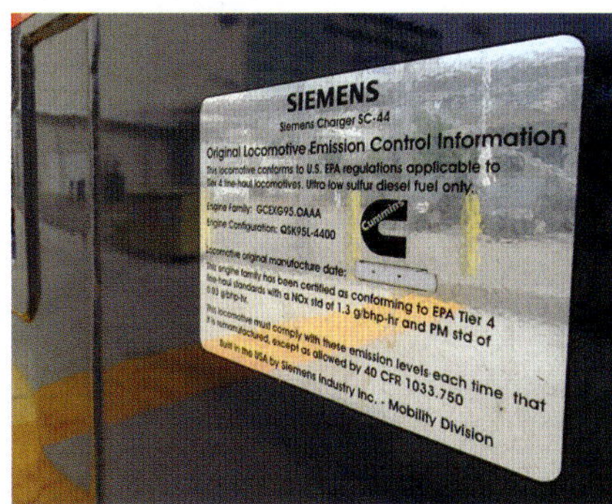

Washington State Department of Transportation (WSDOT) tested an IDOT SC44 in February 2017 and initially purchased eight units, 1400-1408. The first was delivered in 2017 for service on Amtrak Cascades services. This 467-mile corridor connects 18 stations between Eugene, Ore., Seattle, and Vancouver, B.C., with the majority of operating mileage in Washington. The service is jointly funded by the Oregon Department of Transportation and WSDOT, with trains traveling on lines owned and maintained by BNSF, Union Pacific, and Sound Transit.

ALC42: Nos. 300-424 (additional deliveries pending as of 2024)

Recognizing the need to seek replacement for its aging Genesis diesels on long-distance routes, in December 2018 Amtrak announced its order for 75 Charger locomotives — later increased to 125 units — which were scheduled for delivery over an 8- to 10-year span starting in 2022. The first units of the order are designated ALC42 (Amtrak

↑ The 4,400-hp Chargers began replacing 21-year-old F59PHI diesels on California-sponsored routes in 2017. On November 16, 2018, SC44 2109 wears Pacific Surfliner lettering as it leads train No. 774 bound for San Diego at San Clemente, Calif. *Brian Solomon*

← The views at left show the Siemens branding on a Midwest SC44. The builder's plate (bottom) specifies details including their Caterpillar diesel engines and their conformance to the EPA's strict Tier 4 emissions standards. The Chargers are manufactured by the Mobility Division of Siemens in Sacramento, Calif. *Brian Solomon*

Top: The cab interior view of new SC44 Charger 4610 shows its desktop-style controls with multiple computer screens. The engineer's seat is at right. *Brian Solomon collection*

Bottom: New Siemens ALC42 Charger 303 wears Amtrak's Phase VI livery. It was on display in downtown St. Paul as part of the St. Paul Union Depot's Train Days event on June 4-5, 2022. *Chris Guss*

Long-distance Charger, 4,200 hp), and are a variation of the SC44.

Externally, the ALC42 differs from the SC44 in style changes to the streamlined nose section. The ALC locomotives carry larger fuel tanks (2,200 gallons), giving them greater range, plus larger tanks for the engine emissions catalyst liquid. The ALC42 also generates more head-end power — up to 1,000kW, compared to 600kW. The engine itself is derated to 4,200 hp, which conserves fuel and prolongs engine life.

Amtrak's first ALC42, 301, was delivered in February 2022 dressed in a one-of-a kind heritage version of the "Day One" livery; the paint scheme that was originally applied to former Penn Central E8A 4316 (later Amtrak 322), which was little more than a huge version of the arrow logo and white lettering painted over Penn Central black. Five of the first ALC42s were painted in the transitional Phase VI scheme

that features red chevrons on the sides at the back of the largely blue body. Subsequent locomotives debuted the more refined Phase VII livery, designed by Wally Krantz, which features a two-tone blue body and red nose.

The ALC42 made its debut on the *Empire Builder.* The type's usual initial assignments were long-distance trains operating with Superliners, including prominent Western trains as well as the Chicago-Washington D.C. *Capitol Limited* and Lorton, Va.-Sanford, Fla., *Auto Train.* Ultimately, these locomotives are intended to work most of Amtrak's diesel-powered long-distance trains.

New and old Amtrak equipment populate the yard at Philadelphia 30th Street Station. Siemens Charger ALC42 357 was a rare visitor on August 3, 2024. Note the position of the horn on the top of locomotive. Number 726 (left) is a rebuilt GP38-2 (GP38-3), 649 is a Siemens ACS64 electric, and at right, No. 520 is a former GO Transit GP40TC rebuilt to a GP38-H3. *Brian Solomon*

CHAPTER 6

Switchers and non-reve

From classic 1940s switchers to gensets and converted control cars

Alco RS3 138 switches a string of Amfleet cars at South Boston, Mass., on August 11, 1981. The 31-year-old engine was built in August 1950 for New Haven and still wears Penn Central black, albeit with Amtrak lettering. Amtrak operated a wide variety of older power as switchers and work-train locomotives in its early days. Note the lone LRC car to the right of the RS3 — it was one of 10 similar cars leased from the Canadian Government from 1980-1982. *Scott A. Hartley*

nue diesels

Amtrak's former Washington Terminal Alco RS1s work at Washington Union Station on December 14, 1984. Amtrak briefly added these antiques to its roster in the 1980s. Unit 62 at left still wears WT paint and lettering; a few, including No. 44 at right, were painted in Amtrak's Phase III scheme before the whole fleet was retired. *Brian Solomon*

In addition to the road diesels that garner most of the day-to-day attention leading its named passenger trains around the system, Amtrak has also rostered a great variety of other diesel-electric locomotives for menial tasks. This includes fleets of switchers, many of which have labored in relative obscurity at terminals around the system, as well as work-train locomotives employed to haul ballast, rail, and equipment on Amtrak-owned lines.

Amtrak acquired most of these switching and maintenance-of-way locomotives secondhand. In early years, these included switchers and small road diesels from minority builders (mainly Alco) as well as EMD, but recent years have largely seen a focus on EMD products or those rebuilt from older EMD locomotives. In addition, some Amtrak diesels bought new for revenue passenger work were later bumped to switching duties, notably the GE P32BHs.

Since these locomotives tend to be assigned to trains without regular schedules, and they're often out of the public eye, they tend to have been less-often observed and photographed than high-profile road units in regularly scheduled passenger service. Locomotives assigned switching duties have always been common at major terminals, but the operational shift toward standardized consists for locomotive-hauled trains, together with fixed-consist push-pull and self-propelled trains, has reduced the need for switching (and thus switching locomotives).

In several instances, switchers have been painted in unusual variations of Amtrak's standard paint schemes or left to work in the paint from an earlier owner. Owing to relatively light utilization and the durability of older models, switchers have been some of the oldest equipment in regular use on Amtrak, making many of them curious relics worthy of attention.

GE center-cab switchers

Over the years, Amtrak has operated a number of small diesel switchers at various locations around the system. This included several lightweight General Electric center cabs that worked as shop switchers. Units 5 and 9 were 65-ton models while No. 7 was a 45-ton locomotive similar in appearance. The Wilmington, Del., shops have a lone GE 80-ton center-cab, 1100.

Alco S2: No. 746

Among the curiosities on Amtrak's early roster was Alco S2 746. This example of a once-common switcher had previously served as U.S. Army 7110. In

⬆ The Beech Grove shop switcher, GE 45-ton center-cab 7, moves wreck-damaged F40PH 260 for repairs in 1983. This antique was built in May 1941 and acquired by Amtrak in 1977. *Jim Hediger*

⬅ One-of-kind on the Amtrak roster is GE 80-ton center cab switcher 1100, pictured at the Wilmington, Del., shops in June 2016. *Dan Howard*

The last of three RS3m diesels rebuilt by Amtrak was 104, which featured a "chopped" short hood for better forward visibility. It's shown here inside the shops at New Haven, Conn., on March 31, 1984, where it had been rebuilt earlier that year. Alco RS3 117 and a sister unit are at left. *Scott A. Hartley*

"Amtrak's Alco RS3s served as terminal switchers, powered work trains, and occasionally led scheduled passenger trains if road diesels failed."

1974, it was painted in an early version of Amtrak's standard livery with its body dressed in Platinum Mist. For many years it was assigned to Washington Union Station, where it worked alongside Washington Terminal's Alco RS1s. It was retired in 1985, about the same time as the RS1s, which were by then Amtrak property, and eventually scrapped.

Alco RS1: Nos. 44-62

Amtrak took control of the Washington Terminal Company in 1981, assuming operation of the remaining five engines of WTC's fleet of Alco RS1s (built from 1945-1950) that switched cars at Union Station in Washington, D.C. Alco's 1,000-hp model RS1 was first built for Rock Island in 1941, and is significant because it is considered the first true

road switcher and the antecedent of most modern freight diesels. The WTC/Amtrak RS1s were strictly used as switchers.

For several years under Amtrak ownership, the RS1s continued to work in Washington Terminal's dark blue scheme with white lettering, but in June 1984, Amtrak repainted No. 44 in resplendent fresh Platinum Mist using a variation on the Phase III standard scheme. It was soon followed by 46 and 47. However, not long after the repainting began, Amtrak replaced the whole fleet with former Santa Fe SSB1200s. All five RS1s were off the roster by summer 1986. Three later served New York's Tioga Central, including No. 47, which remained in Amtrak paint for many years.

Amtrak SW1s 251 and 252, former Penn Central units, are working at Philadelphia on September 9, 1976. Conrail sold 16 SW1s to Amtrak shortly after CR assumed operation of Penn Central and other properties in 1976. They were initially numbered in the 200 series, but were soon renumbered 730-745 to make room for new F40PHs. Number 251 became Amtrak 738; 252 became 739. *J. David Ingles*

Alco RS3: Nos. 100-144

Among the equipment conveyed to Amtrak upon the creation of Conrail in 1976 were 45 former Penn Central Alco RS3s. The RS3, Alco's standard road switcher of the early 1950s, was rated at 1,600 hp and powered by Alco's 12-cylinder model 244 diesel.

These had variously served PC's component railroads — the Pennsylvania, New York Central, and New Haven — with some still displaying markings of their original owners. A few served in Chicago during the late 1970s, but most were based in New Haven, Conn., where they worked New England lines in various capacities. They served as terminal switchers at Boston's South Station, powered work trains, and occasionally led scheduled passenger trains as rescue locomotives if assigned locomotives failed.

In the 1980s, Amtrak rebuilt and repowered three of its inherited RS3s at its New Haven shop using EMD 12-567B engines salvaged from retired E8As. These were redesignated as model RS3m, wore Phase III livery, and were numbered 104, 106, and 107. The later two were completed in 1981 and 1983 and retained their high short hoods, while 104, rebuilt in 1984, featured a chopped-nose short hood.

Although most of the RS3 fleet was retired after Amtrak received CF7s from Santa Fe in late 1984 (see page 153), the RS3ms survived for several more years. Number 104 was assigned to Washington D.C., while 106 worked at Boston in the early 1980s and later joined sister 107 assigned to Florida terminals.

EMD SW1: Nos. 730-745

Among the equipment ultimately transferred to Amtrak relating to the com-

This Amtrak "pup," No. 743, is former Pennsylvania Railroad SW1 No. 8559. Repainted in Amtrak's Phase III scheme, it is working at Albany-Rensselaer, N.Y., in February 1989. The switcher was one of several former Penn Central units acquired by Amtrak as result of the creation of Conrail in 1976.
Brian Solomon

An odd collection of locomotives, led by MP15 539 and a P32BH, work a ballast train on the former New Haven Shore Line route at Pawcatuck, Conn. *Patrick Yough*

plex transaction that created Conrail was a small fleet of former Penn Central EMD SW1 600-hp switchers. The SW1 was the smallest of EMD's mass-produced switchers and well-suited to industrial trackage and light switching duties at shops and coach yards. Initially, these wore the former PC black scheme, and most were ultimately painted in a variation of the Phase III scheme that made them appear like smaller cousins to F40PH passenger diesels: Platinum Mist body featuring three narrow red, white, and blue stripes, with black roofs and underbodies. The SW1 fleet declined in numbers during the 1980s and 1990s. Unit 737 survived longer than the others, and in 2024 it was reported to have been renumbered to 787 so its old number could be assigned to a GP38-3.

EMD SW1000R: Nos. 790–799

Amtrak bought 10 rebuilt switchers from the Illinois-based National Railway Equipment Company (NRE) in late 1994. Designated as SW1000R, these started life as 1950s-era EMD SW9 and SW1200 switchers built for multiple railroads, including Baltimore & Ohio, Milwaukee Road, Missouri-Kansas-Texas, and Montour. Rated at 1,000 hp, these locomotives are geared for 50-mph operation. They routinely worked at terminals in Washington D.C., Chicago, and California. In 2024, after 30 years of service, only 794 and 796 remained on Amtrak's roster. Unit 794 was repainted in 2018 as a Washington Terminal heritage locomotive, where it was regularly assigned.

Number 551 is a classic EMD end-cab switcher. It was built as an NW2 in 1943 for Santa Fe (2366), and it was among the switchers that the railroad's San Bernardino Shops rebuilt and upgraded to 1,200 hp and redesignated as SSB1200s. It was among the locomotives Santa Fe traded to Amtrak for 18 SDP40Fs in 1984. It's seen at Salt Lake City in July 1991, just two years shy of its 50th year in service. *Brian Solomon*

EMD SW1001: No. 569; SW1500: 540-541

The SW1001 is a model adapted from the 1,000-hp SW1000, featuring a low-profile cab for tight industrial trackage and other places with restrictive clearances. The 569 is former Reading Company 2601, which was originally part of a fleet of 25 units built in late 1973 that went to Conrail in 1976. It was one of three switchers CSX traded to Amtrak in exchange for F40PHs 390 and 395 (which CSX numbered 9992 and 9993 and assigned to its office-car trains). This lone SW1001 is one of the most obscure locomotives on the roster, and has worked a variety of terminals in the East including Albany-Rensse-

Amtrak 567 works Washington Union Station on October 29, 2001. It's only a coincidence that Amtrak's road number also describes the locomotive's prime-mover: EMD's 567-series diesel engine. It was built as an SW1200 for Santa Fe and later rebuilt to an SSB1200. *Brian Solomon*

Amtrak acquired 25 former Santa Fe CF7s in late 1984. Some were painted in Platinum Mist, while others served for years in patched Santa Fe blue and yellow. The 579 is showing its age on November 29, 1992, with areas of blue and yellow showing through the peeling platinum mist paint. Built by EMD as an F7A in 1949, the locomotive was rebuilt in the early 1970s into Santa Fe CF7 2517, and here it's in work-train service in New London, Conn. *Brian Solomon*

laer, N.Y., Philadelphia, and for many year, Washington D.C.

The other two switchers involved in this trade were built as Penn Central SW1500s 9563 and 9572. They later went to Conrail, retaining the same numbers, and eventually became part of the CSX roster with the Conrail split in 1999. Externally, they appear similar to Amtrak's MP15s (see below).

EMD MP15: 530-539

Amtrak bought 10 former Pittsburgh & Lake Erie EMD MP15s in the 1990s for work-train service; some, on rare occasions, have been used as rescue locomotives for revenue trains. The 1,500-hp MP15 was introduced in the

On rare occasions, CF7s worked revenue trains. On March 15, 1986, a labor action on Guilford's Boston & Maine resulted in a detour for train No. 61, the *Montrealer.* This ran south over Central Vermont to Palmer, Mass., where it reversed direction, and was led westward to Springfield, Mass., hauled by former Santa Fe CF7 575. The train has just crossed the Quaboag River on Conrail's Boston Line on the 14-mile run between Palmer and Springfield.
Brian Solomon

"Amtrak acquired its 25 CF7s from Santa Fe in exchange for several SDP40Fs, which Santa Fe converted to freight service."

mid-1970s as a replacement for the popular SW1500, and is more versatile than typical EMD switcher models built from the 1930s through the early 1970s. It blends characteristics of EMD's end-cab switchers with a moderate-horsepower road switcher, and the model's designation infers "multi-purpose." They ride on Blomberg B trucks designed for road service, and Amtrak's units are geared for 65 mph.

Santa Fe SSB1200 (SW-1200M): Nos. 550-567

In late 1984, Amtrak acquired 18 SSB1200s from Santa Fe along with 25 CF7s (see below) as part of a trade for 18 SDP40F road units. The SSB1200 is a 1,200-hp end-cab switcher rebuilt by Santa Fe's San Bernardino, Calif., shops from older model EMD switchers, including 1,000-hp NW2s and SW9s and 1,200-hp SW1200s.

For a short time, some worked in former Santa Fe paint before being dressed in basic Platinum Mist with

Taking a rest between shuffling passenger consists around the Los Angeles Union Terminal, CF7 594 idles in the morning sun while waiting for the *Sunset Limited* on the adjacent track to finish unloading on June 4, 1990. This locomotive was built by EMD as Santa Fe F7A No. 277C and converted into a road switcher at the railroad's Cleburne, Texas shops 20 years later. It sports an unusual interpretation of the Amtrak livery that blends elements of both Phase I and Phase III paint schemes. *Tom Kline*

black/gray tops, running boards, and underbodies with black lettering. These switchers have worked passenger terminals, shops, and coach yards at Los Angeles, New Haven, Conn., Wilmington, Del., Washington, D.C., Miami, Chicago, Albany-Rensselaer, N.Y., Salt Lake City, Utah, and Seattle.

Santa Fe CF7: Nos. 575-599

The CF7 was the product of Santa Fe Railway's Cleburne (Texas) shops. Santa Fe was one of the largest operators of EMD F units, and in the 1970s aimed to rebuild its aging F unit fleet into more versatile road switchers. Following completion of a prototype in 1970, the railroad over the next 7 years embarked on an extensive rebuilding program intended to get another 10 to 12 years of service out of the locomotives. A total of 233 rebuilds were completed through 1978.

The rebuilt locomotives bore no resemblance to F units. They received a new frame and new fabricated hoods to replace the F unit carbody. They retained most primary mechanical and electrical components (with most being rebuilt), including the engine and main and auxiliary generators as well as the control stands, throttles, and air brake controls. Early conversions included cabs that retained the F unit roof contour, while later units featured the

Amtrak GP7 760 — former St. Louis-San Francisco 610 — works the Auto Train facility at Lorton, Va., during preparations for a test run of the new service for Amtrak employees on October 16, 1983. The auto racks are former Auto Train Corp. cars, which were originally built for Canadian National.
Alex Mayes

⬆ A pair of MPI GP15D road switchers waits for the signal at Zoo Junction in Philadelphia on December 15, 2014. Amtrak typically assigns these unusual-looking diesels in pairs to maintenance-of-way trains. *Brian Solomon*

home-built angular "Topeka cab" with a boxy profile that offered greater room for crews. All were rated at 1,500 hp.

In 1984, Santa Fe began disposing its CF7s, including 25 units traded to Amtrak in exchange for SDP40F road units (see Chapter 4). Amtrak renumbered its CF7s 575-599. Some retained their Santa Fe "yellow bonnet" paint schemes for a number of years, while others were painted in Platinum Mist; at least one unit was treated to Phase III style nose stripes. Amtrak assigned its CF7s as switchers at various places around the system, and on occasion CF7s hauled passenger trains in rescue service.

EMD GP7, GP9: Nos. 760-784

During 1977 and 1978, Precision National Corporation (PNC), a company that in the 1960s and 1970s rebuilt and leased older locomotives to a number of railroads, supplied a fleet of rebuilt EMD GP7s and GP9s to Amtrak. These

were primarily for non-revenue service, including work trains and switching. These were initially leased, but Amtrak later purchased them.

Amtrak's locomotives came from a variety of original owners including Chicago & North Western; Louisville & Nashville (including original Nashville, Chattanooga & St. Louis and Chicago & Eastern Illinois engines); Norfolk & Western (including some from Wabash); Rock Island; St. Louis-San Francisco; Quebec, North Shore & Labrador; and Union Pacific.

The first group of GP7s, including 762 and 763 (assigned to Los Angeles as switchers) were dressed in a variation of Amtrak's Phase I scheme: Platinum Mist bodies, black tops and underframes, with red ends and large arrow logos on the sides. Units 760 and 761, initially assigned to Chicago, were painted in a variation of the three-stripe Phase III scheme. Later locomotives were painted in bright safety orange (Equipment Orange) with black lettering — colors that matched ballast hoppers, work-train cabooses, and other maintenance-of-way equipment. These were colloquially known as "Pumpkins" by employees and observers. The orange tended to fade to a pink hue after just a few years.

A late addition was Washington Terminal 80 (ex-Rock Island), which was sequentially renumbered to 784 in 1987. Many of the orange locomotives were assigned to Northeast Corridor

Freshly painted GP38-3 733 and sister 724 lead a loaded concrete-tie train at Landisville, Pa., during upgrading of Amtrak's Harrisburg Line during summer 2024. *Brian Solomon*

terminals where they worked both Amtrak-owned lines and elsewhere. In later years, some of these locomotives were repainted in a very basic livery of platinum mist with black lettering, similar to other non-revenue engines. The fleet gradually diminished in size through the 1990s, with most off the active roster by the mid-2000s.

MPI GP15D: Nos. 570-579

The GP15D is a modern switcher/road switcher built in 2004 by Motive Power Industries of Boise, Idaho. The type is

➡ A pair of Motive Power Industries MP14B genset locomotives (left) idle amid long-distance P42s at the 16th Street diesel shops in downtown Chicago on May 2, 2017. Delivered in 2013 to reduce carbon emissions, these genset locomotives each utilize a pair of 700-hp Cummins diesel-generator sets that are automatically controlled to operate independently or in tandem depending on the load. *Tom Kline*

⬇ This April 2015 view at Washington Union Station could be considered a combined "before and after" photo. Working with National Railway Equipment, Amtrak had five of its classic EMD end-cab switchers (similar to SW1000 796 at right) remanufactured as 2GS-14B "N-ViroMotive" low-emissions locomotives — an example is 597 on the left. *Dan Howard*

powered by a Caterpillar diesel, rated by Amtrak at 1,500 hp. While Amtrak describes its units as GP15D, various industry sources have applied several other model designations. Amtrak assigned these locomotives to a variety of non-revenue maintenance services. They often worked back-to-back in pairs.

EMD GP38: Nos. 720-724; GP38-3: 725 block

Introduced by EMD as part of its new 645-engine diesel line in 1966, the 2,000-hp GP38 proved to be one of the most reliable and popular road-freight locomotives of the mid-20th century. It uses a non-turbocharged, 16-cylinder version of the 645 engine. In 1995, Amtrak augmented its fleet of non-revenue locomotives with five GP38s, Nos. 720-724.

These were later rebuilt to Dash-3 standards (advanced microprocessor controls added) by Norfolk Southern's Juniata Shops. More recently, Amtrak augmented this fleet with another 30 rebuilt GP38-3s from Progress Rail, which were delivered from 2022 to 2024. These are numbered beginning with 725 and expected to reach 754. These feature an advanced electrical system aimed at extending the locomotive service life. Earlier examples are painted in a sharp adaptation of the Phase V livery. However, beginning with unit 740, Amtrak began dressing the locomotives in new standard livery similar to the scheme being applied to new ALC42 (and some P42) road diesels.

Genset locomotives

Genset locomotives employ multiple low-emission diesel-generator sets instead of the conventional arrangement of a single large diesel engine. Each genset is a complete self-contained diesel engine-generator combination. To conserve fuel, reduce carbon emissions, and limit engine noise produced, diesel gensets are automatically controlled by a microprocessor, which only brings the individual gensets online to meet necessary power demands. To even out wear and tear to components, the computer may rotate the use of individual engines. Typical genset locomotives employ two to four gensets.

Between 2010 and 2020, Amtrak sampled several varieties of genset loco-

Here are two views of the first non-powered control unit (NPCU) "cabbage" working *Hiawatha* trains on Canadian Pacific's former Milwaukee Road line in Wisconsin. At top is 90368 in the classic Phase III scheme at the old Sturtevant station on February 2, 2002. Above, 16 years later, the NPCU has been repainted in Phase V livery. It's passing Pleasant Prairie on August 2, 2018. *Brian Solomon*

Top: Amtrak NPCU 90213 leads a Boston-bound *Downeaster* at Dover, N.H., in March 2002. It was rebuilt from F40PH 213 and was one of several NPCUs painted for the Downeaster service operated by Amtrak. *Brian Solomon*

Bottom: On a clear morning in March 2002, NPCU 90213 is on the Boston end of a Boston-Portland *Downeaster* crossing the Merrimac River on the Boston & Maine route at Haverhill, Mass. *Brian Solomon*

motives built by MotivePower Inc. (MPI, a subsidiary of Wabtec) and National Railway Equipment (NRE), assigning them to busy urban terminals. In 2010, it took delivery of two MPI models, one MP14B and an MP21B, 590 and 591. These were examples of the builder's twin- and triple-genset locomotives, rated at 1,400 hp and 2,100 hp respectively. In 2013, Amtrak took delivery of two additional MP14Bs, 592 and 593.

From NRE, Amtrak arranged for rebuilding of five of its older EMD end-cab switchers into 1,200-hp 2GS-14B "N-ViroMotive" genset locomotives. These retained their old road numbers: 597, 599, 792, 793 and 798. The rebuilt locomotives retained their classic end-cab arrangement and ride on standard B-style AAR trucks. These are each powered by a pair of Cummins QSX15 Tier 4 emissions-compliant 600-hp diesel gensets that supply current to four standard EMD D77 traction motors.

NPCU (non-powered control units): 90000-series

Amtrak's Beech Grove shops began converting stored F40PH diesels into cab-control cars by removing the engine, generator, and other control equipment and converting that space into a baggage/storage area (marked by large sliding doors on each side of the body). These conversions — officially called non-powered control units (NPCUs) allowed Amtrak to make economical use of surplus F40PHs. They simplified operations by allowing commuter-rail style push-pull consists, eliminating the need to turn engines and/or trains at terminals. They provided a safe area for head-end crews and provided baggage space for short-haul trains, which freed heritage-fleet baggage cars for other services. These cab/baggage car combinations quickly earned the nickname "cabbages."

The first conversion, 90368 (former F40 No. 368) was completed in 1996, and ultimately 22 units were transformed through former F40PH 406 (retired in 2001 and converted in 2007). Unlike most of the earlier conversions, this one retained its traditional appearance without the large sliding doors, and was equipped to provide head-end power. It was handsomely repainted

At the rear of an Amtrak *Cascade* train is NPCU 90253, sitting in the morning sun awaiting departure with a Talgo Series VI set from Portland Union Station on July 7, 2004. *Tom Kline*

Here's an interior view of the baggage space behind the control cab of NPCU 90413. The unit was converted from F40PH 413, one of six units acquired from GO Transit in 1988. *Brian Solomon*

into the Phase III scheme and from 2011 onward was often assigned to Amtrak promotional trains, including its display train that toured the system. Until 2024, it retained its traditional number, when it was renumbered 90406 to allow for continuous numbering of new Siemens ALC42s.

The NPCUs have been regularly assigned to push-pull trainsets used on the *Downeaster,* Midwestern services from Chicago including the *Hiawatha* (Milwaukee) and *Wolverine* (Detroit) corridors, California's *Pacific Surfliner*, and Amtrak *Cascades* service in the Pacific Northwest.

CHAPTER 7

Siemens Cities Sprinter ACS64 634 leads *Keystone* train No. 651 as it leans into the restrictive curve at Gap, Pa., on September 12, 2024. The 600-series ACS64s entered revenue service in 2014, and are routinely assigned to Keystone services, which have carried 600-series train numbers since the Penn Central era. On rare occasions the locomotive numbers and train numbers neatly coincide. *Brian Solomon*

Electric locomotives

From classic GG1s to modern Siemens Mobility Cities Sprinters

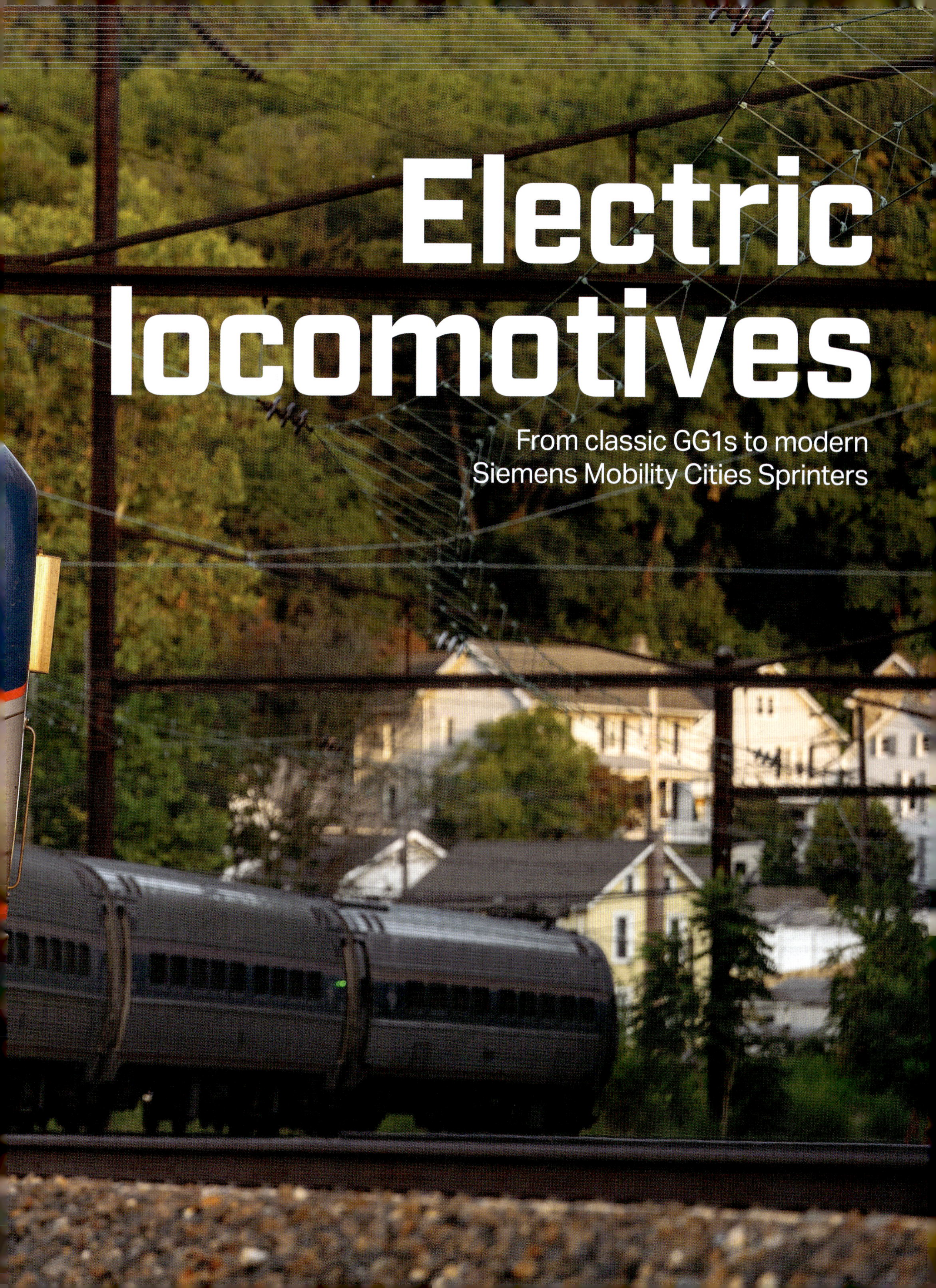

Amtrak's fleet of overhead-wire electric locomotives may seem relatively small compared with its fleet of diesel-electrics. However, although electrified territory represents only a small fraction of Amtrak's national service area, the intensively used electrics are high-profile, high-tech machines powering frequent, fast trains that carry a significant portion of Amtrak's national ridership.

It was rare to find three GG1s on one train. These venerable electrics were nearing the end of their long tenure in this June 10, 1980, photo. They're hauling train No. 152 at Burr Road Tower at Bridgeport, Conn. This was a power-balancing move: Two of the GG1s were needed at New Haven to bring another train west. The three had recently been renumbered back into the 4900 series to make room for the new AEM7s that would soon replace them. *J.W. Swanberg*

Amtrak inherited electric passenger operations from Penn Central over the Northeast Corridor (NEC). This included trains operating via New Haven's pioneering high-voltage AC overhead between its Connecticut namesake city and New York City by way of the famous Hell Gate Bridge, as well as on Pennsylvania's New York-Philadelphia-Washington and Philadelphia-Harrisburg (Pa.) overhead routes.

One of the big changes that occurred as a consequence of the Penn Central debacle was the transfer of ownership of Northeast Corridor properties, including significant portions of the Boston-Washington and Philadelphia-Harrisburg line to Amtrak. (Among the

exceptions were key electrified portions of the former New Haven in Connecticut and New York that had been conveyed to state agencies.)

Owing to the persuasive lobbying efforts of Amtrak's then-president, Paul Reistrup, as part of the creation of Conrail, Amtrak in 1976 purchased from Conrail key portions of the NEC necessary for its passenger services. In conjunction with this change was legislation authorizing $1.6 billion in Federal funds for Northeast Corridor improvements, which began in March 1977. This resulted in extensive infrastructure upgrades and much-needed maintenance.

Locomotive overview

At the time of Amtrak's assumption of intercity passenger services in 1971, former Pennsylvania Railroad GG1 electrics remained the core of Penn Central's electric fleet. In its early years, Amtrak continued to rely on these streamlined steam-era relics — some of which dated to the 1930s. The GG1s were augmented in the mid-1970s by a fleet of 26 boxy General Electric E60CHs/E60CPs, and ultimately supplanted in the early 1980s by a fleet of Swedish-designed, EMD-built AEM7s.

Extension of NEC electrification in the late 1990s saw commencement of electric operations all the way to Boston

⬆ In their later years, Amtrak's remaining E60MAs were largely assigned to long-distance trains on the Northeast Corridor between Washington and New York. This March 2001 view at Philadelphia's 30th Street Station finds a pair of E60MAs on a heavy northbound long distance train — an uncommon sight, as these electrics typically worked singly. *Brian Solomon*

940
940
Amtrak
940
Amtrak

in 2000, which required significant additions to the electric fleet. This included upgrading some AEM7s, the purchase of high-speed trainsets for *Acela Express* service (Chapter 2), and the addition of 15 new high-horsepower HHP8 locomotives using the same propulsion technology and exterior design.

After more than 30 years of intensive service, the AEM7 fleet needed replacement. In October 2010, Amtrak ordered 70 modern electrics based on Siemens Vectron platform, adapted to meet North American standards and refined for high-speed service on the NEC. Designated as Amtrak Cities Sprinters, model ACS64, they were assembled domestically between 2013 and 2016 by Siemens Mobility at its Florin plant in Sacramento, Calif. Since retirement of the last AEM7s in 2016, the ACS64 has become Amtrak's primary electric locomotive, working alongside the *Acela Express* trains in daily service.

Amtrak's electrics have largely been assigned to passenger trains, although at various times they have sometimes served in work train service, including GG1s and E60s. In 1987, Amtrak bought eight former Pennsylvania E44 electrics from NJ Transit for work-train service. These were briefly assigned numbers 500-507, and at least one of these was painted in Platinum Mist with black lettering.

GG1: 900 series, 4900 series

Pennsylvania Railroad's GG1 — arguably the most recognizable electric locomotive in North America — was among the locomotives that Amtrak inherited from Penn Central. This icon of American railroad design was a much-admired machine that since the 1930s had represented the face of PRR's great New York-Washington electrification. In their day, the GG1s were the largest fleet of mass-produced streamlined electrics in North America.

The design was developed in 1934 to overcome the failings of PRR's earlier boxcab-type electric locomotives. Pennsylvania had electrified its Philadelphia suburban services beginning in 1913, using overhead catenary at 11,000 volts AC at 25Hz — the standard established by the New Haven in the previous decade. The success of this operation led the railroad to announce ambitious plans in 1928 to electrify mainline operations on its heavily traveled routes connecting New York, Philadelphia, Baltimore, and Washington, D.C. It was the most extensive project of its kind in the United States, and four decades later it became the core of Amtrak's busy Northeast Corridor.

The Philadelphia services had been operated with a fleet of class MP54 multiple-unit cars. However, mainline electrification required developing new electric locomotives. Initially, PRR created several classes of boxcab electrics

⬆ Car inspector George Myer removes the blue flag from the cab of GG1 926 at Harrisburg, Pa., during a blizzard on February 6, 1978. On a day when flights are grounded and highways are clogged and treacherous, the trains keep rolling. The blue flag is the most restrictive signal on the railroad. It's designed to protect workers on, under, or between rolling stock, and the flag may only be removed by the employee that displayed it. *Jim Bradley*

⬅ The AEM7, a product of ASEA and EMD, first entered revenue service in 1980 and proved to be a reliable, capable locomotive. Here AEM7 940 leads a northbound Northeast Direct train across the Susquehanna River at Perryville, Md., in November 1997. *Brian Solomon*

using various wheel arrangements with rigid wheel bases that mimicked the arrangements of its most successful standardized steam locomotives. These, however, had a number of engineering flaws, including the end-cab design — which exposed the crew to collision danger — and lacked the power needed for big trains.

In trying to find a solution, PRR tested a New Haven EP-3 electric that benefited from a 2-C+C-2 articulated wheel arrangement. The railroad worked with Baldwin and Westinghouse in developing a pair of experimental electrics, classes R1 and GG1, each of which used a similar semi-streamlined body with an elevated, centrally positioned cab. The prototype GG1 with the 2-C+C-2 arrangement was deemed superior during testing.

In *Classic Trains,* author Hampton C. Wayt wrote that the locomotive's early design was largely the work of Westinghouse's industrial designer, Donald Dohner, who established the basic shape of the locomotive. Later, to improve the appearance of the production GG1, PRR hired industrial-design pioneer Raymond Loewy, who implemented a host of changes that included using a modern welded body in place of the riveted construction of the prototype. Loewy also introduced the elegant livery with Brunswick Green (dark green locomotive enamel) body and five gold pinstripes.

Powerful and fast, the GG1 proved to be a remarkably capable locomotive. Between 1935 and 1943, the Pennsylva-

Next stop, New York Penn Station! On January 18, 1981, E60CH 969 (later renumbered 607) races west through Rye, N.Y., leading train No. 151, the *Shoreliner*. Mechanical issues and tracking problems kept the big electrics from achieving their hoped-for performance. *Walter E. Zullig, Jr.*

nia acquired 138 GG1s, many assembled at its own Juniata Shops. As built, they were 79'-6" long with 57"-diameter driving wheels and weighed between 460,000 and 470,000 pounds. They were rated for a continuous 4,620 hp output, but could develop much higher power in short bursts, which enabled rapid acceleration. A lone GG1 was capable of leading a 20-car passenger train at 90 mph. The GG1s handled the majority of PRR's intercity passenger traffic on the New York-Washington and Philadelphia-Harrisburg routes.

When Amtrak assumed operation of Penn Central's long distance passenger trains in 1971, the GG1 remained a rugged workhorse locomotive in electrified territory. Penn Central's control of the New Haven in 1969 had extended the GG1s' operating territory east from New York to New Haven, Conn. However, by this time the fleet had at least a quarter century of hard service behind it, and the locomotives were showing their age. PRR had begun retiring GG1s in 1966, and many of the oldest units had been transferred to freight service.

Amtrak initially acquired 30 GG1s from Penn Central, mostly "newer" locomotives built between 1940 and 1943. When PC was melded into Conrail, Amtrak acquired an additional 10 units. Amtrak introduced a new numbering scheme for GG1s, initially in the 900 series. In theory, this meant a three-digit number by dropping the "4" from the PRR/PC 4900-series units; in practice, the numbers only occasionally corresponded because Amtrak wanted a solid number block between 900 and 929. In 1979, near the end of the GG1 era, Amtrak renumbered its remaining 900-series GG1s back into the 4900s to make room for new AEM7s.

Most Amtrak GG1s initially wore Penn Central black with white lettering and numbers. Beginning with No. 926

This rendering shows an artist's vision of the first General Electric E60CP with a train at Secaucus, N.J. It's depicted having just exited the North River Tunnels from Penn Station against a mid-1970s New York skyline. Although the actual E60s were never painted in the Phase I scheme, they would have looked impressive. *Trains magazine collection*

Amtrak 900, the first AEM7, was assembled by EMD in 1979 at La Grange, Ill., using ASEA electrical components and a Budd-built body. It's shown while testing with the EMD dynamometer car at Whitford, Pa., on the former Pennsylvania main line. Photos of this pioneer electric leading trains in revenue service are rare, as the locomotive was famously destroyed in a wreck at Chase, Md., on January 4, 1987.

Dan Cupper collection

(ex-PRR 4933) in 1973, six GG1s were painted in a unique adaptation of Amtrak's first standardized livery. These featured black underbody, Platinum Mist bodies, a single broad Loewy stripe in blue, red patches wrapping around the nose-ends above the stripe, and "Amtrak" printed in large black block lettering on the sides.

Between March and May 1977, under the direction of Friends of the GG1, a group under the wing of the National Railway Historical Society organized by Howard Serig, Amtrak repainted GG1 4935 into the classic original Loewy scheme. It was among the first examples of a locomotive dressed in "heritage paint" and came complete with PRR period lettering. Amtrak 4935 was dedicated in Washington D.C., on May 15 of that year in a ceremony attended by Loewy himself.

In addition to working the Northeast Corridor, Amtrak's GG1 fleet also led trains on the Keystone Route — the former Pennsylvania main line west of Philadelphia to Harrisburg — and for a short time hauled the Washington-Harrisburg section of the *Broadway*

Limited over the Port Road line, which hugs the Susquehanna River to Perryville, Md.

Although it was initially expected that the arrival of modern E60C/CH electrics in the early 1970s would replace the venerable GG1, in fact it was the large numbers of AEM7s several years later that finally allowed Amtrak

to retire its GG1 fleet. The venerable electrics made their final runs in 1981.

General Electric E60CP, E60CH: Nos. 950-976 (later 600 series)

Among Amtrak's first orders for new locomotives were 26 General Electric six-motor electrics intended to replace the high-mileage, aging former Pennsylvania GG1s. And, like Amtrak's early diesel orders, Amtrak's electrics were for a modern C-C (two six-axle trucks) freight design adapted to Amtrak's requirements — the single-ended 5,100-hp E60C that GE built for Arizona's coal-hauling Black Mesa & Lake Powell.

On May 14, 1977, borrowed French National Railways' Alstom-built electric X996 received Phase II paint and Amtrak lettering at the Wilmington, Del., shops for its brief visit to the United States. A pair of GG1s are also in the shop for repairs. *Trains Magazine collection*

On Election Day 1992 (November 3), a *Metroliner*—Train 107—is whisked through Newark, Del., toward Washington behind AEM7 902. The compact electric has more power than needed to lead this four-car express at more than 100 mph. *Brian Solomon*

Amtrak's resulting E60CP and E60CH were longer (71'-3"), double-ended, and designed for multivoltage service (former PRR 11kV/25Hz and anticipated new installations at 12.5kV/60Hz). They were officially rated at 6,000 hp, but could produce almost 10,000 hp short-term, which meant rapid acceleration. The two variations reflected the transitional arrangement for heating and lighting on Corridor trains at the time: The E60CPs (950-956) had steam generators, and the E60CHs (957-976) had head-end (HEP) power to match the new Amfleet cars ordered at the same time.

The first of the fleet, E60CP 950, was completed in late 1974; the remainder followed throughout 1975. The locomotives cost approximately $692,000 each and were among the first locomotives dressed in Amtrak's broad-striped Phase II livery to match the Amfleet cars. Modern E60s leading matched consists of Amfleet cars presented a stark contrast to black GG1s leading mixed consists of battle-worn, hand-me-down cars.

Although designed for a maximum 120-mph speed, a derailment during testing revealed potential flaws in the six-wheel freight trucks used on the E60s. This was significant, as it limited the E60s to 85 mph in revenue service. Although the E60s were still suitable for hauling heavy long-distance trains on the NEC, Amtrak recognized that further study of modern electric locomotive designs was necessary to obtain the locomotives needed for high-speed services. These studies ultimately resulted in the AEM7 (see the next section).

In their early years, the E60s worked alongside the GG1s they were intended to replace. In 1983, Amtrak sold off some its E60CHs — 966 and 968 were sold to the Navajo Mine in New Mexico, and a group of them was leased (and later sold) to NJ Transit, which used them to replace its own GG1s on the North Jersey Coast route.

In the mid-1980s, Amtrak began rebuilding and renumbering its remaining E60s. This resulted in regearing passenger-service locomotives for 90-mph operation. Units 600-610 were redesignated as E60MA, while 620-621 retained the E60CP designation, and these were largely assigned to work train service and limited to 80 mph.

In their last years, the E60s sported a variation of the three-stripe Phase III livery and typically worked heavy long-distance runs on the NEC. The last 600-series units were retired in 2003 and 2004. Unit 603 has been preserved at the Railroad Museum of Pennsylvania in Strasburg.

AEM7: Nos. 900-953

When the GE E60s proved to be unsuitable for high-speed service — and thus unable to replace the GG1s — and

Delivered in 1988, AEM7 947 was one of six built for Amtrak's final order for the distinctive electric. It is one of a handful of AEM7s painted in the short-lived Phase IV scheme that roughly coincided with the Northeast Direct branding of the mid-1990s. It glides west at Shaws Cove in New London, Conn., in October 2002. *Brian Solomon*

⬆ Number 916 was reaching the end of its service life when it glided through Bryn Mawr, Pa., leading a westbound *Keystone* on December 4, 2014. It was retired a year after this photo was made, and scrapped in the spring of 2016. *Brian Solomon*

with the lack of other practical domestic designs, Amtrak looked to Europe, where commercial manufacturers had perfected modern, fast electric locomotives. During 1976 and 1977, Amtrak imported a Swedish-built Allmänna Svenska Elektriska Aktiebolaget (ASEA, later part of ABB) four-axle model Rc4. This was modified for Amtrak's service, painted in the Phase II scheme, and numbered X995.

About the same time Amtrak also imported a six-axle SNCF (French National Railways) CC 21003 built by Alstom, numbered X996. Both were used in comparative testing on the Northeast Corridor. The French electric wasn't well suited to American track geometry, but Amtrak was pleased with the Rc-4. It performed very well in cold weather and at high speeds, and seemed well-suited for Amtrak's intended service.

In the mid-1960s, ASEA had pioneered the application of thyristor semiconductor rectifiers for sophisticated motor control. Thyristor control offered several distinct advantages over older systems. Notably, it enabled continuous stepless motor control and individual traction-motor control that maximized output and minimized wheel slip. This gave a locomotive greater tractive effort while reducing maintenance costs in part by eliminating mechanical electrical switching equipment.

Following several years of experimentation, in 1967 ASEA introduced the class Rc1 locomotive on Swedish State Railways (SJ). These were considered the first commercial production locomotives to employ thyristor motor control. Models Rc2 and Rc3 followed, but the significantly more advanced Rc-4, introduced in 1975, incorporated a variety of improvements, namely ASEA's sophisticated Pressductor wheel-slip technology. In semi-technical terms, the system senses torsional

← Amtrak AEM7 916 works at speed at the back of a *Keystone* push-pull set gliding through Leaman Place in Paradise, Pa., in March 2009, This minimalist scheme of the mid-2000s was in stark contrast to the bold, patriotic paint that characterized the locomotive's appearance in the 1980s. *Brian Solomon*

↓ Sunset on a classic: For more than 30 years, AEM7s leading matched consists of Budd-built Amfleet cars were *the* standard train on the Northeast Corridor. In the twilight — and the twilight of its career — 936 races east at Niantic, Conn., in February 2010. *Brian Solomon*

Amtrak AEM7AC 918 is typical of the AEM7s that were rebuilt with polyphase alternating-current traction. It was nearing the end of its service life when pictured leading a westbound *Keystone* on the former Pennsylvania four-track main line near Bryn Mawr, Pa., on July 1, 2014.
Brian Solomon

axle oscillation and is able to correct it on individual axles, transferring power to other axles before the slip causes a loss of adhesion. This made the Rc4 exceptionally powerful and capable of rapid acceleration and high speeds, despite its relatively compact size and light axle weight.

Amtrak worked with American suppliers to build a fleet of electrics that adapted the Rc4 for North American service. The overall design of the new locomotive, including the electrical system and trucks, was the work of ASEA, which licensed its American partner, EMD, to assemble the new locomotives. They were designated AEM7 (ASEA-Electro-Motive 7,000 hp). Budd was contracted to build the carbody shells, which to meet American high-speed safety requirements had to be made significantly stronger (and as a result heavier) than the Swedish Rc design. Prior to Amtrak's testing the Rc4, EMD had already established a relationship with ASEA in collaborating on the design of two modern heavy-electric experimental demonstrators for freight service. Known as the GM6 and GM10, these had tested on Penn Central and Conrail in the mid-1970s.

In revenue service, the AEM7 was designed to deliver 5,695 hp continually (7,000 hp peak) and operate at a maximum speed of 125 mph. They were 51'-8" long with 51"-diameter wheels —

operated AEM7s singly and in pairs. A lone unit was generally restricted to hauling eight Amfleet cars due to HEP capabilities.

To coincide with the start of regular electric operations between New Haven and Boston, between 2000 and 2002 Amtrak remanufactured 29 AEM7s at its Bear Shops in Wilmington, Del. Significant work focused on replacing the traditional DC traction system with modern asynchronous AC traction similar to that employed by the original Acela Express HST sets. With this, the locomotive automatically senses differences in voltage/frequency drawn from catenary and appropriately aligns the tap changer to send current through the main transformer. The transformer works with a rectifier to convert AC voltage to 2,000 volts DC. Inverters then convert voltage back to a form of AC current to power traction motors, auxiliary systems, and train HEP. The

Number 945 survived in service longer than many other AEM7s, even though it was not among the locomotives upgraded as AEM7ACs. Toward the end of its career this battle-worn beast was showing its age. It suffered from a worn suspension, which made it unpopular with engineers who begrudgingly tolerated its bouncy ride — which was especially bad when passing through crossovers. Today Amtrak 945 is preserved at the Illinois Railway Museum at Union, Ill. *Brian Solomon*

much larger than standard freight locomotive wheels. They were equipped with HEP, and each had two Faiveley style pantographs, one at each end of the locomotive. When built, the AEM7 was believed to have the highest horsepower-to-weight ratio of any locomotive in the U.S.

Between 1980 and 1982, Amtrak received two orders totaling 47 AEM7s (900-946) at an estimated cost per unit of $2.5 million. As planned, these served as primary motive power on the Northeast Corridor between Washington, New York, and New Haven. In the late 1980s, Amtrak ordered seven more AEM7s, 947-953, in part to replace units destroyed in accidents. Amtrak

electrical system has four inverters, one for each traction motor, plus a fifth auxiliary inverter that delivers three-phase 480V current through an auxiliary transformer for train HEP and other equipment (traction-motor blowers, water and oil pumps, radiator blowers, and the main air compressor).

The upgraded locomotives were equipped with two common forms of electric braking; rheostatic (dynamic braking), where current generated by traction motors is directed into grids to be dissipated as heat, and regenerative braking, where braking current is fed back into the overhead catenary. Upgraded locomotives were designated AEM7AC to distinguish them from unmodified units. The rebuilt locomotives were easily identified by the significant addition of electrical equipment in metal cages atop the locomotive roof. Both traditional AEM7s and ACs had the same traction capabilities and were functionally compatible with one another. The AC traction system was aimed to provide greater reliability and lower maintenance costs.

Amtrak's small fleet of Bombardier-Alstom HHP8 electrics featured a double-ended, dual-cab design that was similar in appearance to the High Speed Trainset power cars permanently assigned to Acela Express service. Here HHP8 No. 661 glides across the Norwalk River at South Norwalk, Conn., on November 3, 2002. They were normally assigned to work conventional consists on the Northeast Corridor. *Brian Solomon*

Amtrak HHP8 663 leads train No. 98, the Miami-New York *Silver Meteor,* on the Northeast Corridor toward Philadelphia at Ridley Park, Pa., on March 13, 2009. The 8,000-hp electrics were built by the Bombardier-Alstom consortium in 1998-1999. *Dan Cupper*

After retirement from electric service, HHP8s 691 and 692 were experimentally converted to NPCU-style cab cars and renumbered 9750 and 9751. They're at 30th Street in Philadelphia (sans pantographs) in August 2024. *Brian Solomon*

⬆ The Siemens Mobility Cities Sprinter ACS64 made its revenue debut on February 7, 2014, when class leader unit 600 led Northeast Regional train No. 171 from Boston to Washington. The sparkling-clean locomotive is shown passing Milford, Conn., on its run. Several months later, 600 was named in honor of former Amtrak president David Gunn. *Brian Solomon*

➡ Amtrak Cities Sprinter 611 kicks up the snow as it blitzes through Branford, Conn., leading Northeast Regional train No. 161 (Saturday and Sunday only) bound for Washington D.C. from Boston on January 10, 2015. *Brian Solomon*

Also in early 2000s, the fleet was repainted in spartan variations of the phase V livery; the locomotive bodies were dressed in Platinum Mist, the tops painted blue with a thin red sill stripe, and charcoal for the lower body and running gear. Generally, Amtrak's logo was positioned on the sides below the cab windows. Some AEM7s had logos on the front but many did not, resulting in a no-frills, utilitarian appearance.

By the mid-2000s, a quarter century after their debut, Amtrak still had 52 AEM7/AEM7ACs on its active roster, with 35 to 39 needed to cover daily assignments. In the 2010s, as the new Siemens Cities Sprinter ACS64 electrics were delivered, Amtrak began withdrawing both versions of AEM7s from active service. They made their final runs in spring 2016. Most were scrapped or stored (at Davisville, R.I.). As of 2024, three have been preserved: 915 by the Railroad Museum of Pennsylvania in Strasburg, Pa., 917 by the Danbury Railway Museum in Connecticut, and 945 at the Illinois Railway Museum in Union, Ill.

Bombardier-Alstom HHP8: Nos. 650-664

Between 1999 and 2001, Amtrak bought 15 high-horsepower locomotives built by the Bombardier-Alstom consortium, designated HHP8. These double-ended, dual-cab locomotives shared styling and technical attributes with the Acela Express HST power cars (see Chapter 2) and were built during the same period. Their delivery was timed to coincide with completion of Northeast Corridor electrification to Boston.

611 611
AMTRAK

Train No. 98, the *Silver Meteor* (Miami-New York), includes a selection of Viewliner equipment on its head end as it races through Levittown, Pa., on December 19, 2015. Commuter rail operator SEPTA has since replaced this station's low-level platforms with modern high-level platforms. *Brian Solomon*

The Northeast Corridor in transition: On January 10, 2015, new ACS64 601 leads Northeast Regional Train 88 through Metro-North's recently opened Fairfield Metro Station at right as a set of 1970s-era Metro North M2 "Cosmopolitan" multiple-units pause to collect passengers. The M2s shared trackage with ACS64s for just a few years; they ran off their final miles in Metro-North's reserve fleet and were withdrawn at the end of 2018. *Brian Solomon*

These extremely powerful (8,046-hp) four-axle locomotives measured 67'-1" long, weighed 222,000 pounds, and had a maximum designed speed of 135 mph. They used the same propulsion system as the Acela HSTs to draw current from the multitude of AC electrification standards on the NEC route.

The HHP8s augmented the fleet of AEM7s, and ultimately allowed Amtrak to retire the remaining 1970s-era GE E60 locomotives. While often assigned to Amtrak's regional services, they also routinely powered the long-distance trains that operate on the NEC, including the *Crescent, Silver Meteor,* and *Silver Star,* owing to these trains' long, heavy consists.

Colloquially the HHP8s were known as "Hippos," which was both a word play on their model designation and vaguely descriptive of their shape. Although powerful, they reportedly suffered from low reliability, which contributed to their retirement after only about 15 years of service. The HHP8s were renumbered 680-694 to make room for the new Siemens Mobility ACS64 electrics delivered in 2014 and 2015, but Amtrak quickly stored and then retired the relatively small HHP8 fleet.

After retirement, 691 and 692 were stripped of their pantographs and converted to experimental NPCUs (non-powered control units) in 2022 and 2023. Number 691 was initially renumbered 90691, following the pattern of earlier NPCUs, but was later renumbered 9750; 692 became 9751. Success with this type of conversion may ultimately allow for the retirement of 1960s-era Metroliner control coaches.

Siemens Mobility Cities Sprinter: Nos. 600-670

Amtrak's ACS64 — also known as the Amtrak Cities Sprinter — is based on Vectron's Eurosprinter electric locomotive. The body features modern monocoque construction (similar to contemporary passenger diesels) that complies with North American crash-worthiness standards as mandated by the Federal Railroad Administration. Safety features include a minimum 800,000-pound buff strength, full-width anticlimbers, push-back couplers, and cab-crumple zones. The ACS64 features several distinct characteristics including its front-end styling, along with Amtrak's Advanced Civil Speed Enforcement System (ACSES) control and signaling system, required for use on the NEC.

The Vectron locomotive platform was introduced in 2010, with Amtrak placing the first ACS64s in service in 2014. Adapted for Amtrak service, the ACS64 measures 66'-8" long, rides on

Amtrak 606 was the first ACS64 that was briefly wrapped in a special scheme to promote the change from Pepsi to Coke in dining and café cars. On December 22, 2019, the locomotive races along the Northeast Corridor with train No. 175 at Andalusia, Pa. *Patrick Yough*

44"-diameter wheels, and weighs 215,537 pounds. It's designed to haul up to 18 Amfleet passenger cars at 125 mph while delivering up to 1 megavolt-ampere (MVA) for head end power.

The AC-traction locomotive employs Siemens' state-of-the-art SIBAS 32 three-phase control system. This advanced electrical design uses IGBT (insulated gate bipolar transistor) semiconductor high-voltage inverters that draw current from overhead wire, regulate it, and feed it to modern three-phase AC traction motors. The electrical system automatically senses differences in supplied electricity, enabling it to draw power from the three different catenary standards in use on the NEC.

Siemens details the locomotive's propulsion and drive system in its promotional materials: "The propulsion unit consists of a pinion hollow shaft drive with the traction motor mounted directly to the truck frame by rubber elements. The gear is axle-mounted, riding on the wheelset with the other side mounted to the motor case by a reaction rod. Two multiple-disc clutches are installed between traction motor and gear to allow movements between these two components. One clutch is located directly between the motor and hollow shaft, the second clutch is located between the hollow shaft and pinion." The Cities Sprinter design utilizes the same style of center-pin integral welded-frame trucks also employed by Siemens Mobility's Charger diesel-electrics.

Sophisticated regenerative braking feeds 100% of braking power back into the electrical supply system via the overhead catenary, making more efficient use of electricity than older systems. The locomotives are rated at 6,702 hp continuous with 8,579-hp

maximum short-term output. A pair of inverters supply HEP, which offer high capacity with built-in redundancy.

The ACS64s were numbered 600-670, but without a unit 666. In summer 2013, new 601 was sent to the U.S. Department of Transportation Testing Center near Pueblo, Colo., for extensive testing. This milestone event was observed by Amtrak president Joseph Boardman, FRA Administrator Joseph Szabo, and Siemens Rail Systems president Michael Cahil. Testing on the Northeast Corridor had begun May 2013. In one of these tests, an ACS64 leading a short train brought it up to 125 mph with three of its four motors isolated.

The model officially entered revenue service on February 7, 2014, when unit 600 led Boston-Washington Northeast Regional train No. 171. As the ACS64s were delivered, they quickly supplanted the tired, aging fleet of 1980s-era AEM7s and the Alstom HHP8s on trains working Boston-New York-Philadelphia-Washington. The type is routinely used in push-pull service on the Pennsylvania-sponsored *Keystone* trains between Philadelphia and Harrisburg. In recent years, this handsome locomotive has been the standard Amtrak electric on all locomotive-hauled and push-pull sets in electrified territory, except for Acela Express trains that operate with the specialized HST trainsets (see Chapter 8).

Most ACS64s are painted in an adaptation of the phase V scheme. Unit 642 wears a special paint scheme commemorating America's veterans. A few have been briefly wrapped in temporary advertising liveries and other short-lived special schemes. Unit 600 was later named to honor former Amtrak president David L. Gunn.

Wearing the commemorative scheme designed to honor America's veterans, ACS64 642 leads eastbound *Keystone* Train 652 at Leaman Place, Pa., in October 2023.
Brian Solomon

CHAPTER 8

Passenger cars

"Heritage Fleet" hand-me-downs have given way to specialized cars of many types

This May 2024 view looks northeast at Amtrak's Chicago car facilities immediately south of Union Station. A remarkable variety of Superliner, Siemens Venture, Viewliner, and Horizon cars can be seen together. *Chris Guss*

Amtrak began operation with wildly diverse collections of passenger cars acquired from private railroads, most of which in the early years were still painted for their previous owners. Amtrak gradually thinned the ranks of these cars, retiring or adapting them during its "rainbow era," and later converted many for use in what became known as its "Heritage Fleet." Amtrak quickly recognized, however, that it would benefit from a fleet of uniform car designs — built to modern standards — to meet its specific requirements.

This resulted in the design and acquisition of a large number of new cars, first in the form of single-level Amfleet and bi-level Superliner cars, and later in the design of the Viewliners and Horizon cars. In the 1990s, California led the way in investing in specialized fleets of modern bi-level cars for operation on its state-sponsored Amtrak services, while in the Pacific Northwest, fleets of distinctive Talgo trains were bought for Amtrak Cascades service. Most recently, next-generation Siemens Mobility Venture and Aero fleets are being acquired for regional and long-distance services, both to replace half-century-old Amfleet equipment and to increase Amtrak capacity to allow ridership growth.

Rainbow fleet

When Amtrak took over, it had its choice of approximately 3,000 passenger cars from the fleets of the 18 railroads that conveyed their operations to the new unified carrier. Since Amtrak's ini-

In December 2018, Viewliner II Baggage car 61020 is at New Orleans in the consist of a *Polar Express* holiday train. This photo nicely shows the contrast in profiles between Amtrak's Viewliner and Horizon cars (ahead of the baggage car). *Brian Solomon*

Amtrak acquired a dozen former Chicago & North Western long-distance service, gallery-style, bi-level push-pull cars that it operated on Illinois-supported services. In July 1981, train No. 380 — the Champaign-Urbana to Chicago *Illini* — passes Bement, Ill., on Illinois Central Gulf trackage. *Mike Abalos*

tial routes represented a drastic scaling back of operations, it only required a fraction of the available cars to operate its trains. It selected approximately 1,200 of the best and most appropriate available cars to create what became colloquially known as its "rainbow fleet," which described the colorful collections of cars dressed in schemes of several private railroads.

The majority of these were post-World War II, lightweight streamlined cars, primarily built by American Car & Foundry, Budd, Pullman-Standard, and the St. Louis Car Company. A large portion of cars were from Western railroads (Burlington Northern, Santa Fe, Southern Pacific, and Union Pacific) plus cars from pre-merger predecessors of Penn Central and Seaboard Coast Line.

Day coaches were the most common car type. In addition, the initial fleet included 50 lounge cars, 140 dining cars, almost 290 sleepers and 244 Slumbercoaches, plus a variety of upscaled cars including 90 domes, more than 70 Santa Fe Hi-Level cars, and many luxury coaches.

Many cars were 20 to 25 years old and had rolled millions of miles in service. Some had received excellent maintenance over the years, but many had suffered effects of deferred maintenance and repairs. By the 1960s railroads knew the end of passenger service was coming, and weren't going to invest any more money into passenger cars than what it took to keep them rolling.

These cars were all designed for operation using the traditional steam-heat system with steam provided by a boiler on the locomotive. Steam was used for air conditioning on some cars as well. Although head-end power (HEP) using electricity was common on commuter trains, it would take significant time (and money) to apply this to the long-distance fleet.

Although compatible in terms of couplers, brake lines, and other essential equipment, a challenge was that individual cars had been built to various specifications according to the requirements of their original owners. In some situations, cars had been customized for intended operation on a specific train. As result, there was a great variety of different car configurations and styles. Although this delighted observers and thrilled some avid train riders, it left Amtrak with a variety of compatibility problems and other operational headaches.

➡ California car 6852, the *Elysian Park*, is a business-class coach painted and assigned to the *Pacific Surfliner*. On August 2, 2016, it's trailing Genesis P42 206 at Santa Susana Pass. The car has a capacity of 77. *Brian Solomon*

Heritage upgrades

The winter of 1976-1977 brought extremes in snow and cold temperatures, severely hampering steam-heating equipment and capacity on many Amtrak trains. This led Amtrak to convert the best of its traditional passenger cars to HEP to make them compatible with its new Amfleet cars. The conversions created what became known as the Heritage Fleet.

Most of this work was accomplished during the late 1970s and early 1980s at Amtrak's Beech Grove (Ind.) Shops. Conversions included many coaches, baggage cars, standard 10-6 (10-roomette, 6-double-bedroom) sleepers, lounge-diners, and dome cars. Many cars received substantial additional refurbishment in addition to HEP equipment. While this project significantly extended the service life of the refurbished cars, it also resulted in a mass retirement of older equipment when many distinctive and unusual early cars, such as round-end observation cars, were removed from service.

An Amtrak brochure from 1990 described its remaining Heritage Fleet. It listed 136 coaches, noting that these had largely been Pennsylvania Railroad, Santa Fe, Southern Pacific, and Union Pacific cars that had been modified to accommodate mobility impaired passengers. Coaches were largely of the classic corridor arrangement, with pairs

⬇ In a time-honored tradition, a baggage handler and station agent off-load arriving passengers' luggage from the westbound *Sunset Limited* at El Paso, Texas, on June 3, 1990. Two carts of departing passengers' luggage and freight await loading. *Tom Kline*

of reversable seats opposite each other separated by a central aisle. Seating capacity ranged from 44 to 88, with two toilets per car.

There were also a dozen Vista Dome coaches that had total seating for 66 passengers, of which the 20 elevated dome seats were unreserved. Popular with passengers during the day, these also offered unrivaled views in the evening. Passengers could take in nocturnal panoramas, watching as towns and cities passed and automatic block signals dropped from green to red. Three full-length Budd dome lounges had been rebuilt for *Auto Train* service in 1983. These had 90 seats, with a bar and lounge area on the lower level and an electric piano in the dome area.

Food-service cars included 28 full diners, 15 buffet cars with seats for 32 passengers, several cafeteria-lounge cars (including four designated as "Le Pub" cars for *Montrealer* service), and four "table cars" reserved for the *Auto Train*. As late as 2004, two dozen of these cars remained on the roster.

Overnight cars included 23 Slumbercoaches with accommodation of up to 40 passengers, and a fleet of 91 sleepers, the majority of which were 10-6 arrangement. These were largely postwar Budd-built stainless steel cars with fluted siding.

Of the Heritage Fleet, the baggage cars, diners, sleepers, and crew dorms survived the longest. Most were finally retired when their Viewliner II replacements entered service after 2015. A half-dozen of the classic style of cars remain for display purposes on Amtrak's Anniversary Train.

> "Of the Heritage Fleet, the baggage cars, diners, sleepers, and crew dorms survived the longest."

The early 2000s were an eclectic period on Amtrak, as a great variety of equipment coexisted in different paint schemes. At 12:17 p.m. on September 30, 2000, train No. 43, the westbound *Pennsylvanian,* rolls downgrade through Cassandra, Pa., on Norfolk Southern's former Pennsylvania main line. Leading was P42 26 in Phase IV paint, followed by a sister wearing the Phase III scheme, followed by three material-handling cars, three Horizon coaches, a lone Amfleet car, and an array of freight equipment including RoadRailer trailers at the rear. *Brian Solomon*

Amfleet

In 1973, Amtrak made a bold move by placing a huge order for modern passenger cars with the Budd Company. New cars were needed to augment and supplant the fleets of aging cars inherited at Amtrak's startup. These were intended to help accommodate an expected surge in ridership stemming from rising gasoline costs, as well as improve the reliability and appearance of its busiest corridor services.

Amtrak worked with Budd to create passenger cars patterned after Budd's high-speed self-propelled Metroliner cars, but for locomotive-hauled service. During early planning the new passenger car was provisionally called the "Metro-Shell." However, Amtrak engaged the marketing firm of Needham, Harper & Steers, which dreamed up the name "Amfleet" to describe the new design and original names for the different car configurations: Amcoach, Amcafe, Amclub, and Amdinette.

Amfleet broke from traditional passenger-car design, following Metroliner cars by employing a tubular design with curved sides for strength. These offered greater interior space by making better use of the loading gauge. This structure and Budd's welded, fluted stainless steel construction made for an exceptionally strong, durable car capable of withstanding high-speed crashes with minimal damage, while their bodies were free from the effects of corrosion.

Instead of perpetuating the obsolete steam heat and lighting systems of Amtrak's inherited cars, Amfleet was designed for operation with head-end power (HEP) provided by the locomotive. This offered greater reliability, as HEP was less prone to a variety of operational problems associated with steam heat — namely steam pressure dropping toward the ends of long trains and the need to maintain adequate water supplies for steam.

Locomotives supply 480V, three-phase AC stepped down by transformers on the cars to 220V or 120V as required for on-board heating, lighting, and other accessories.

Although HEP was an advancement, in its early years Amtrak had to deal with compatibility problems between Amfleet cars and existing equipment. Initial plans were for Amfleet to work medium-distance corridor services, with little need to operate mixed consists with older cars. However, in practice, it wasn't that simple. Amtrak was forced to provide HEP power cars in situations where locomotives were not HEP equipped, and steam generator units to allow HEP-equipped locomotives to haul traditional steam-heated trains.

Amfleet cars were designed for 120-mph operation. They ride on inside-bearing trucks (36"-diameter wheels), giving them a distinctive appearance as the wheel faces are exposed. The trucks incorporate an air-suspension system to provide a smooth, quiet ride, and they're equipped with disc brakes.

The cars featured many innovative interior features for the period, including audio equipment and electrical connections for a public-address system throughout the train, self-contained chemical toilets, and electrically operated interior and exterior doors. Some Amfleet features emulated airline travel, including the use of retractable tray tables, reclining seats, and individually controlled overhead lights.

The doors between cars were opened with large rectangular pushbutton switches at hand level as well as ground level "kick panels." This made travel between cars much easier, eliminating the need for passengers to wrestle with older manually operated doors. Unfortunately, the electric doors proved chronically unreliable and were a source of frequent maintenance. The kick panels

Top: The *Floridian* (train No. 53) sports a vintage Budd Vista Dome at Hollywood, Fla., on February 17, 1975. Prior to Amtrak, Budd domes were rare on trains in the Southeast. Amtrak reassigned domes to a variety of its popular trains serving cities where they had not previously operated.
Walter E. Zullig, Jr.

Bottom: In the steam-heat era, car 5335 wearing fresh Amtrak paint awaits boarding at Pittsburgh.
Paul Roth

On May 21, 1972, the eastbound *Broadway Limited* still had two un-repainted Union Pacific cars in its consist as it departed Chicago for New York. Former Baltimore & Ohio sleeper-lounge *Dana* (No. 3251) adorns the rear of the consist. Notice the collection of cars in the former Pennsylvania coach yard in the background, including several former Norfolk & Western cars, among them an ex-Wabash *Blue Bird* dome coach.
J. David Ingles

These images of Train No. 96, the *Vacationer*, paused at Wildwood, Fla., on February 20, 1973, demonstrate the great variety of passenger cars that worked together during Amtrak's rainbow years. Many still wear the schemes of former owners. Note the former Chesapeake & Ohio car lettered for Seaboard Coast Line and the Great Northern car inherited from Burlington Northern. *Two photos: Walter E. Zullig, Jr.*

On September 9, 1971, a little more than 4 months after Amtrak assumed operations, its *Texas Chief* runs with ex-Santa Fe Budd-built stainless steel cars (including Hi-Level cars and a full-length dome) led by leased Santa Fe F units. Although it looks almost identical to Santa Fe's pre-Amtrak train, the visual tip-off is the location: Santa Fe served Chicago's Dearborn Station, while this train is approaching Union Station. Note also the assortment of baggage-express and Flexi-Van container cars on the post office tracks in the background.
George W. Kowanski

were especially problematic and suffered from excessive wear and from water damage that resulted in short circuits.

Vestibules are located at both ends of each car, which — combined with electric doors — allow for rapid loading in areas with high-level platforms. The cars measure 85'-4" long, 10'-6" wide, and 12'-8" tall, a profile that allow them to operate without restrictions across the network.

As-built, there were five distinct Amfleet car configurations. There were two varieties of Amcoaches: a high-capacity 84-seat car and the more comfortable 60-seat version, which offered greater leg room for long distance services. There were three types of food

In September 1975, the westbound *Empire Builder* pauses at Havre, Mont., for a service stop en route from Chicago to Seattle. The train carried a variety of cars including Budd Vista Domes and full-length domes bought in the 1950s by multiple railroads.
George W. Kowanski

service/lounge cars: Amcafe, with a snack bar and coach seats; Amclub, with a snack bar and a mix of coach and club seats; and Amdinette, with eight booths plus coach seats. Each of these were often reconfigured during their service lives.

As built the cars had interiors decorated in classic mid-1970s style. Amcoaches featured rich hues of burgundy, burnt orange, and pink and floral patterns on seats. Amclubs emphasized dark reds.

Amtrak placed its first Amfleet order in October 1973 and the first cars entered revenue service on August 7, 1975, working the *Statesman* between Washington and Boston. Ultimately, Amtrak placed four orders for the original Amfleet design (later described as Amfleet I), totaling 492 cars: 271 84-seat Amcoaches, 90 60-seat Amcoaches, and the remainder food-service cars, including a pair of specialized lounge cars built for the *Montrealer*. These orders were completed by June 1977.

Over the years, the Amfleet cars have served as the core of Amtrak's corridor fleets, rolling up millions of miles per car. At various times, Amtrak has reconfigured, reallocated, and refurbished the fleet. In the early 1980s, some cars were assigned to a dedicated fleet specially adorned for Metroliner service named Metroliner Coach, Metroliner Club, and Metroliner Dinette.

In the late 1980s, Amtrak begin rebuilding the fleet for push-pull service, which resulted in completed cars being renumbered from the 20000 series to the 40000 series. This work took more than 20 years to complete. In 2001, Amtrak began a wide-scale program to refurbish Amfleet I equipment. This coincided with the Northeast Regional rebranding, resulting in another mass renumbering of cars in the 80000 series.

In 2012, 90% of the original fleet remained serviceable. In 2017, another fleet-wide refurbishment began that included adding a new style of seat cushions, replacing carpeting, installing new low-energy reading lamps, updating curtains for business class, and improving restrooms.

A decision to phase out Amfleet I cars was announced in 2018, as Amtrak ordered fleets of new cars from Siemens Mobility. The most significant new equipment will be the Airo trainsets, which are intended to begin replacing Amfleet I cars on Northeast Corridor and some state-sponsored services in 2027, by which time these veteran cars will have seen a solid half-century of service.

Amfleet II

The success of the initial Amfleet cars and the need for additional modern cars led Amtrak to order a revised car design from Budd in 1980. These new

"The first Amfleet cars entered revenue service on August 7, 1975."

The Washington-bound *Montrealer*, train No. 61, glides through South Norwalk, Conn., on June 25, 1986. At the back is heritage sleeper 2903 *Pacific Bend.* It's a common variety of 10-6 car (10 roomettes, 6 bedrooms), built by Budd in 1950 for Union Pacific. It was one of several dozen similar heritage cars that Amtrak converted for operation with head-end power (HEP). *Brian Solomon*

February 5, 1977, finds a pair of Duluth, Missabe & Iron Range SD9s leading train No. 762, the southbound *Arrowhead,* at Grasston, Minn. Finding SD9s in passenger service was a rare event, especially in the Amtrak era. The DM&IR engines filled in because of a motive-power shortage attributed to ongoing problems with Amtrak's new SDP40Fs. At the rear of the consist is former Burlington dome coach 9743. Today, if Amtrak ran this consist, it could charge premium fares for the experience! *Steve Glischinski*

cars, called Amfleet II, incorporated a variety of minor changes to make them better-suited for longer-distance trains. Notable differences included larger side windows, more leg room with just 59 seats per coach, sliding windows in the vestibule doors, and vestibules at just one end of each car.

During 1981, Budd delivered 125 Amfleet II coaches and 25 lounges. These Amlounges featured a central snack bar with 17 lounge seats at one end and 32 table seats at the other.

The first Amfleet II coach, car 25001, was displayed at Budd's Red Lion, Pa., plant in November 1981 for inspection by Amtrak's officers and members of the press.

Superliners

Western long-distance trains have been among Amtrak's most popular services since it began operations in 1971. When Amtrak was looking to re-equip its western fleet, it wanted to make the most of the ample clearance standards afforded by main lines in the region, and opted for a new double-deck design patterned on Budd's Hi-Level cars first built for Santa Fe in the 1950s. The Santa Fe cars, which were an integral part of Amtrak's Heritage fleet, had debuted on the *El Capitan* in 1954 and resulted in additional orders in 1956 and 1964.

In 1975, Amtrak placed a large order with Pullman-Standard for bi-level cars called Superliners. This remarkable new design offered many advantages over traditional single-level cars. They had more space, resulting in greater comfort and higher capacity, and the large windows and higher seating position on the upper level allowed passengers much better views of passing scenery.

Superliner consists resulted in shorter trains, making better use of short sidings and stations with short platforms, which was especially important at terminals where platform space was at a premium and wasn't easily expanded without complicated and expensive changes.

The first car, 34013, was completed in October 1978, and the first train to be fully equipped with the new cars was the Chicago-Seattle *Empire Builder.* By 1981, P-S had completed 284 Superliner cars. They were the last passenger cars

built by the historic Chicago-based manufacturer.

Among the distinctive attributes of the design were the low center entrances that enabled easier boarding from traditional low-level platforms (instead of high end doors at vestibules that required steps). These make better use of space inside the car, provide easier access for mobility-impaired passengers, and for loading the train with provisions. Connections between cars is on the upper level.

Superliners measure 85 feet long and stand 16'-2" tall — 8 inches taller than Santa Fe's cars — and, depending on specific configuration, weigh about 157,000 pounds. The original fleet included two types of coaches totaling 150 cars. In their early configurations, standard coaches featured 62 seats on the upper level and 15 on the lower level, plus specialized accommodations for mobility-impaired passengers, a women's lounge, and restrooms on the lower level.

Baggage-coaches originally had up to 78 seats on the upper level (later reduced to 62 to allow more leg room), with the lower level allocated to a women's lounge, restrooms, and storage space. Amtrak later configured a third coach arrangement (11 cars) that it called a Coach Snack Car. These had 62 upper-level seats with a snack bar on the lower level.

Pullman-Standard built 68 Superliner sleepers. These featured a variety of accommodations with total capacity for up to 44 passengers. There were economy bedrooms with 10 on the upper level, plus five upper-level deluxe bedrooms each equipped with lower double beds and an upper bed, of which four of the units could be combined into "bedroom suites" to enable larger groups to travel together. Additionally, on the lower level was a large family-sized bedroom and a bedroom designed to accommodate mobility-impaired travelers.

The Superliner fleet included 39 full-service dining cars featuring seats for 72 people with an all-electric kitchen on the lower level. One of the delights of the Superliner fleet has been the glass-topped observation cars, originally called Sightseer Lounges. Always

The *Vermonter* (St. Albans, Vt.-Washington, D.C.) crosses the Quaboag River at Palmer, Mass., on February 6, 1996. This day train was introduced in 1995 to replace the overnight *Montrealer,* and was among several Northeast trains that carried specially decorated baggage cars. Baggage car 1801 was built for Northern Pacific in 1956 by Pullman-Standard. *Brian Solomon*

Top: Amfleet I regional coach 82723 is part of the consist on Northeast Regional train No. 163 at Old Saybrook, Conn., in February 2010. For almost five decades, Amfleet coaches have been the most common type of car in the fleet, and they've served as the workhorse on the Northeast Corridor and other regional services. *Brian Solomon*

Bottom: Amfleet I business class car 81544 rolls through New Haven, Conn., on June 26, 2012. These cars have seating for 60, offering more leg room than standard coaches. *Brian Solomon*

popular with travelers, these feature an upper level with swiveling chairs and lounge-style seating with exceptionally large windows that were the next best thing to Budd's original Vista Domes. The lower level hosts a food service area with restaurant style seating.

Since their introduction, Superliners have served as the core of Amtrak's Western fleet. They were later assigned to some Eastern runs as well, including *Auto Train* and the *Capitol Limited*. Owing to historically restrictive clearance on key eastern routes, Superliners cannot be assigned to trains originating or terminating in Boston and New York, among other principal stations.

In 1991, Amtrak augmented the Superliner fleet by ordering additional new cars from Bombardier, built to the Pullman patterns. These were called Superliner II cars, and they were built in Barre, Vt. Externally, these cars exhibited a few minor changes, including slightly different side fluting, and came with Phase IV striping. Superliner II cars included 38 coaches with 75 seats (34100 series); 55 sleepers (32000 series) and deluxe Auto Train sleepers (32500 series); 30 dining cars (38000 series); and 25 lounges with glass-covered observation-style windows (33000 series) and crew-dorm sleepers (39000 series). These cars are typically operated

together with the older Superliners on long-distance trains.

Delivery of the Superliner IIs allowed retirement of many older cars in the Heritage Fleet, including some popular types such as traditional dome cars. Most of those had at least four decades of service, and many were not equipped with retention toilets, which were mandated in the 1990s.

To simplify operations, Amtrak tends to assign standardized configurations to Superliner trains. This enables forwarding consists between routes to improve equipment utilization while minimizing the need to switch consists at terminals.

Horizon Cars, 53000-54000 series

By the late 1980s, passenger service was growing and Amtrak again needed more standard passenger cars. Its Heritage Fleet coaches were approaching the end their service lives, but the historic 20th-century American passenger car suppliers had exited the business. The simplest solution was to follow the lead of commuter rail operators, many of which had bought standard cars from Canadian manufacturer Bombardier, a growing transportation supply company that had acquired significant passenger car patents from Budd and Pullman-Standard.

⬆ An Acela Regional train crosses the former Pennsylvania Railroad bridge over the Schuylkill River in Philadelphia behind AEM7 941 on March 28, 2001. This was a transitional period for Northeast Corridor branding: The locomotive wears the early 1980s Phase III scheme, while most of the Amfleet cars are in the short-lived Acela Regional variation of the Phase V paint scheme. The bridge is actually reinforced concrete faced with sandstone, designed to resemble earlier stone-arch structures. *Brian Solomon*

On May 28, 1999, F40PH No. 414 leads an eastward Empire Service train on the Water Level Route at Guy Park, N.Y. The five-car train of Amfleet I cars has an Amcafe in Phase III paint, bracketed by pairs of coaches wearing Northeast Direct branding. *Brian Solomon*

Amfleet I coach car 62684 is part of a five-car consist on train No. 55, the southbound *Vermonter,* on the former Boston & Maine near Greenfield, Mass. The view nicely shows the car type's inside-bearing high-speed trucks, which leave the wheel faces exposed. *Brian Solomon*

In 1988, Amtrak placed an order for 104 medium-distance cars (86 coaches, 18 food service) from Bombardier. These were adapted from the design of Pullman-Standard's Comet I commuter car. They had first been first built for New Jersey-subsidized suburban service on Erie Lackawanna in the early 1970s, with similar cars built by Bombardier in the 1980s for MBTA, Metro-North, NJ Transit, and SEPTA. Amtrak called this new fleet its Horizon cars.

The cars were built at Bombardier's Barre, Vt., plant, and were delivered during 1988 and 1989 at a cost of slightly less than $1 million each. As a

In 2008, Amtrak introduced its Northeast Regional brand, which replaced the Acela Regional branding on Amfleet-equipped Northeast Corridor trains. Amfleet I car 43362, at New Haven, Conn., was originally an Amdinette and is now identified as a Café. Amtrak's many food-service cars have undergone several configuration changes and renumberings over their long careers.
Brian Solomon

fleet, they were the first cars bought without Federal subsidy, although a portion of the order was funded by California's Caltrans.

Consistent with commuter rail designs, the Horizon cars featured spartan interiors with only basic comfort systems, but they had more spacious seating than typical commuter cars. They used a variation of the General Steel Industries outboard-bearing truck, similar to that found on Metroliner and Superliner cars.

The coach and food cars each had subclasses. The three types of coaches (54000 series) included a standard 82-seat coach; a 76-seat coach with extra baggage storage; and an ADA-compliant coach with 72 seats. There were two types of food cars (53000/53500 series). Both featured a centrally located food-preparation area (which notably lacked exterior windows), but they varied in the amount of table seating.

During the 2000s, Amtrak overhauled most of the Horizon fleet, resulting in changes to seating configurations, accessibility, and food service arrangements that corresponded with several renumberings.

The bodies of the cars are a light-color brushed metal. In their early years they featured two variations of the Phase III livery; some wore the commonly applied narrow three stripes, and others had broader striping. In the 1990s, many of the cars were repainted in variations of the Phase IV scheme.

Less common than Amfleet, the Horizon cars were routinely assigned to state-supported corridor trains including California's Oakland-Bakersfield *San Joaquins* and San Jose-Sacramento *Capitols*, Chicago-based *Hiawatha* services, Illinois and Michigan services, and *Cascades* in the Pacific Northwest. In addition, they have been used on long-distance services to augment other equipment, as well as seasonal and special trains such as the California-based *Reno Fun Train*.

Viewliner

The Viewliner is an Amtrak car design specifically developed for operation on lines with low vertical clearances — primarily in the East — that are too restrictive for hi-level Superliner equipment. The Viewliner designs were intended to replace obsolete Heritage fleet cars; specifically sleeping cars, diners, and ultimately baggage cars.

Viewliner development involved unusually long gaps between building prototypes, accepting designs, and finally manufacturing cars for regular service. With input from Budd, Amtrak's Beech Grove Shops built two prototype sleepers and a lone prototype diner in 1987 and 1988. These exhibited many of the features that would be associated with Viewliner design, including the characteristic paired rows of side windows, which in the sleeping car design offer upper windows on the top bunk in sleeping compartments and in dining cars offer cathedral-like natural illumination.

In December 1992, after almost 5 years of testing, Amtrak finally authorized Boise, Idaho-based Morrison-Knudsen to build 50 Viewliner sleepers (62000-62049). The order was finally completed in 1995 and 1996, when they were delivered by American Passenger Rail Car Company (Amerail) — successor to M-K's railcar construction division.

In the long interval between prototype and production, a variety of minor design changes were implemented to the Viewliner sleeping car. With total rated capacity of 30 passengers, these feature a dozen standard bedroom compartments (roomettes) — six on each side of the car — two larger bedrooms, and a handicap-accessible bedroom. Viewliner sleepers are 85'-4" long, 14'-0" tall, and weigh 140,500 pounds.

The Viewliner offers passengers a distinctly different travel experience then Amfleet or

This telephoto view of the eastbound *California Zephyr* at Solitude, Utah, in September 1996 offers a comparison between the various Superliner and Superliner II car profiles and Amtrak paint schemes. *Brian Solomon*

other coach cars. The standard bedroom compartment can accommodate two adult passengers using facing seats with a central retractable table. Overnight the seats are folded to create a lower bunk, and the upper bunk is lowered and locked into place. Standard bedrooms include a folding sink and non-enclosed toilet. Additional toilet facilities are at one end of the car.

Amtrak has routinely assigned these cars to Eastern long-distance trains (more than 750 miles), including the Boston-New York-Chicago *Lake Shore Limited*, New York-Washington-Chicago *Cardinal* (which traverses CSX's former Chesapeake & Ohio route via Clifton Forge, Va.), New York-Florida *Silver Star* and *Silver Meteor,* and New York-New Orleans *Crescent*. In the 1990s, Viewliners offered overnight accommodations on the Boston-Washington-Newport News *Twilight Shoreliner,* some of which were

Superliner interiors feel bright and modern. These bilevel cars have been a hallmark of Amtrak's Western trains and are noted for their large windows and glass-top skylights, with different arrangements of seating to allow travelers to congregate and enjoy the passing scenery. At right is the view from the upper level of Superliner dining car 38030 as it rolls westward on Train 1, the *Sunset Limited*—one of the oldest passenger train names in use by Amtrak. At left is the interior of the upper level on a Superliner lounge on the *Sunset Limited.* *Brian Solomon*

specially decorated for the run.

Maintaining the Viewliner theme, in their early years each of the initial Viewliner (later known as Viewliner I) sleeping cars carried a themed name ending in "view." These were organized in alphabetical order through their numbers, with the first in the series (62000) being *American View,* followed by 62001 *Atlantic View* and originally concluding with 62049 *Winter View.* Prototype sleeper 2301 was rebuilt, renumbered 62091, and named *Eastern View* in 2001.

In one of those classically convoluted car-renaming scenarios, after just a few years, this car was again stored but after a decade rebuilt into a theater-

Resembling an N scale model, a lone F40PH leads a four-car Superliner consist on Train 27 — the westbound Portland section of the *Empire Builder* — at Wishram, Wash., on July 2, 1994. *Brian Solomon*

style business car confusingly named *American View.* In the meantime, Amtrak had quietly dropped the original Viewliner I names, but from 2015 onward began renaming the cars after rivers, again following alphabetical order with 62000 becoming *Altamaha River* and 62049 becoming *Pearl River*.

Viewliner II

Although Amtrak had anticipated acquiring a fleet of dining cars, lounges, and baggage/crew dorms built using the Viewliner pattern, decades passed before the design was revived to fulfill this vision. It wasn't until 2010 that Amtrak ordered additional equipment, which would be known as Viewliner II.

Left: *Pacific Surfliner* passengers view the scenery of California's Santa Susana Pass from a Superliner café lounge along Union Pacific's former Southern Pacific Coast Line in August 2016. Right: A Superliner diner in its original scheme is in the *California Zephyr* in 1989. *Two photos: Brian Solomon*

Horizon coach 54555 is in a consist of similar equipment on a Chicago-bound *Hiawatha* at Sturtevant, Wis., on August 1, 2018. Built by Bombardier in 1989, Amtrak's Horizon coaches (54500-54585) have seats for 69 passengers in their modern configuration. *Brian Solomon*

Trains meet at 16th Street Station at Oakland, Calif., on April 18, 1993. The Los Angeles-bound *Coast Starlight* with Superliners is at left, while a Sacramento-bound *Capitol* led by an F40PH is changing crews. This scene soon changed: Amtrak moved its facilities to Emeryville in August 1993 and later opened a new station at Oakland's Jack London Square. The tracks were relocated in the mid-1990s to make room for the I-880 freeway. *Brian Solomon*

In June 1989, brand-new Horizon coach 54040 and a sister car rest at Conrail's yard at Palmer, Mass., where they had been delivered by the Central Vermont for interchange. The cars, built by Bombardier at Barre, Vt., were delivered to Amtrak using a CV-Conrail routing. *Brian Solomon*

Amtrak ordered 130 Viewliner II cars from Spanish railroad supplier CAF (Construcciones y Auxiliar de Ferrocarriles, S.A.), which assembled the cars to Amtrak's specifications at its facilities in Elmira, N.Y. The order included 25 sleeping cars (62500-62524), 25 diners (68000-68024), 55 baggage cars (61000-61069), and 25 combined sleeping car-baggage cars (69000-69009), known as "bedroom cars" or baggage/dorms.

The first car was delivered in 2014, and the new baggage cars entering service began working on long-distance trains in 2015. Viewliner II sleepers continued the River-series names, with 62500 named *Portage River* and the last in the series, 62049, dubbed *Westfield River* (after the gently flowing waterway in the Berkshires of Massachusetts — the route of the Boston section of the *Lake Shore Limited* and one of the oldest continuously operated main lines in America). These sleeping cars offered improved features compared with the original Viewliners, including contemporary interior design with better lighting and climate control.

Viewliner II diners are named alphabetically after state capitals, starting with 68000 *Albany* and concluding with 68024 *Tallahassee*. Ironically, many of these cities are not currently served by Amtrak, while some that are — such as Sacramento — are not represented.

California Cars

Since the mid-1990s, state-sponsored California corridor services have largely employed the purpose-built double-deck California Cars patterned after the Superliners. Their initial design and funding was facilitated by public ballot initiatives in 1990 that authorized public investment in rail expansion.

They were designed and styled for a consistent profile with the EMD

Amtrak

On March 9, 1997, The westbound *Reno Fun Train* descends Donner Pass near Alta, Calif., with an unusual consist of Horizon cars on either side of a Budd full-length dome. The train had operated seasonally between Oakland, Calif., and Reno, Nev. *Brian Solomon*

F59PHI diesels that were ordered around the same time to power the trains. Among the advantages of these cars are high capacity and ease of boarding at low-level platforms, made possible by multiple automatically controlled doors that don't require the vestibule steps or traps typical of most traditional single-level equipment. Although California Cars were specifically designed for California services, they are compatible with other Amtrak cars and have routinely operated with Superliners.

California Department of Transportation (Caltrans) originally ordered 88 cars from Morrison-Knudsen in February 1992. However, Morrison-Knudsen was reorganized during the cars' production, which complicated delivery. Ultimately the order was completed by M-K's successor, Amerail. Caltrans scaled back its order to 66 cars: 14 cab-control cars (8300-series), 86-seat coaches that, on the upper level, feature engineer's controls compatible with F59PHI locomotives; 32 standard 90-seat coaches (8000 series); six

coach/baggage cars (8200 series) with seats for 84 passengers; and 14 food-service cars (8800 series). For all car types, the majority of passenger seating is on the upper level, with additional seating, toilets, and other facilities on the lower level.

In 2000 and 2002 Amtrak and Caltrans expanded this fleet, buying additional California Cars from Altstom known as Surfliners. This enabled assembly of nine five-car trainsets for expanded *Pacific Surfliner* service (San Diego-Los Angeles-San Luis Obispo), while making cars available for other Amtrak California routes. Eight sets were funded by Amtrak and one by California.

These were colorfully painted in white and multiple shades of blue to resemble the hues of the Pacific Ocean and named after key California natural landmarks including beaches, canyons, and parks. In their original configuration these sets included a 6800-series business-class car, two 6400-series coaches, a 6300-series coach/café, and a 6900-series cab car (with coach and baggage space).

Talgo

Amtrak's operation of Talgo articulated train sets is part of a complex connection between a Spanish railroad supply company and American railroads that dates back more than 75 years. The Talgo name is an acronym that blends the names of key men behind the distinctive train: inventor Alejandro G. Omar and businessman José Luis de Oriol y Urigüen, plus a description of the train itself, Tren Articulado Ligero Goicoe-

> "Horizon, Viewliner, and Superliner cars were all designed to replace Heritage cars on various routes, trains, and services."

On February 8, 2002, a 54500-series Horizon coach on a Chicago-bound *Hiawatha* displays a Yahoo ad as it rolls through Sturtevant, Wis. *Brian Solomon*

Amtrak
Viewliner

chea-Oriol. Omar was the genius that envisioned Talgo in the late 1930s by blending several innovative concepts. He refined those ideas during the 1940s into a sophisticated, unconventional passenger train that ultimate found a variety of international applications.

Talgo employs a low-profile (less than 11 feet tall above railheads), short-length, lightweight tubular car design with multiple cars coupled in fixed articulated sets, with cars sharing common wheels. Significantly, the wheel pairs do not share common axles, but are independently attached to the car body. This arrangement offers a low center of gravity with minimal wheel resistance (resulting in less wear) that permits high-speed operation with gentler effects from centrifugal forces.

Talgo built an early prototype in Spain in the late 1940s, then contracted American manufacturer ACF to produce several trainsets: three for RENFE (Spanish National Railways) plus an American demonstrator, which ACF sent on a public tour of U.S. railroads. As a result, in the mid-1950s Boston & Maine, New Haven, and Rock Island acquired experimental Talgo trains for revenue service at time when light-

Top row, left to right:

← Horizon coach interiors are utilitarian but comfortable, with 69 reclining seats. *Brian Solomon*

During 1987-1988, Amtrak's Beech Grove Shops built a lone prototype Viewliner I diner, 8400, and a pair of prototype Viewliner sleeping cars. The diner was later named *Indianapolis*. *Dan Cupper*

Amtrak Viewliner sleeping car 62048 *Wayside View* was specially decorated for service on the *Twilight Shoreliner*. *Brian Solomon*

A Viewliner baggage car and sleepers are at the head end of train No. 98, the northbound *Silver Meteor* (Miami-New York City), as it passes Ashland, Va., on CSX's former Richmond, Fredericksburg & Potomac main line on June 8, 2015. The cars have a unique angled side profile. *Brian Solomon*

↓ Here's an interior image of Viewliner diner 68006 *Charleston*, built in 2017, as it worked on train No. 19, the southbound *Crescent*, in December 2018. These modern purpose-built cars feature kitchen facilities at one end and room for up to 44 passengers at the other. Art deco styling is a nod to the early stainless-steel streamlined cars of the 1930s and 1940s. *Brian Solomon*

AMTRAK RAIL-FREIGHT

Amtrak's 41000-series 48-foot RoadRailer trailers were largely assigned to mail service, as this one at Chicago, Ill., in February 2003. They were typically attached to the rear of long-distance passenger trains. The RoadRailer trailers didn't require complicated yard facilities, they offered low tare weight, and had a streamlined, low profile that was well-suited to operation with passenger cars. *Brian Solomon*

During the late 1990s, a funding crisis resulted in a congressional mandate that Amtrak achieve financial self-sufficiency. Part of Amtrak's solution was to develop a high-priority express freight business, using cars carried on its regularly scheduled passenger trains. For a few years, Amtrak's express business was a visible component of its Network Growth Strategy, which included movement of U.S. Mail traffic.

To handle greater amounts of express, it acquired fleets of passenger-compatible freight equipment to augment its fleets of baggage cars and the 150 material-handling cars bought new from Thrall in the 1980s. New freight equipment included a fleet of RoadRailer trailers, which used a lightweight design well-suited to being carried at the back of passenger consists. Many trailers were painted in the Phase IV livery, which was predominantly Platinum Mist with blue and red stripes. As its business grew, Amtrak also leased some white (non-branded) RoadRailer trailers.

This traffic grew quickly in its first few years, resulting in some long-distance trains hauling a half dozen or more RoadRailers. Amtrak also invested in a fleet of former Southern Pacific 50-foot boxcars (70000-70049) rebuilt to work in passenger consists, plus two orders of new passenger-train-compatible 60-foot boxcars (71000-71299). Some of the boxcars were painted forest green, while others were in Platinum Mist Phase IV and V schemes.

While it developed a significant freight business and extended some passenger trains to better serve key freight hubs, Amtrak's freight-hauling phase proved short-lived as it resulted in a variety of problems. In some instances freight movements lengthened passenger schedules and required extended station stops. More detrimental were delays caused by mechanical problems or switching moves. Not only did delays affect on-time performance and annoy passengers, but the emergence of Amtrak as competition for time-sensitive traffic angered its host railroads. Amtrak's freight business was largely discontinued by the end of 2004.

On November 5, 2001, the eastbound *Three Rivers* from Chicago looks more like a freight train than an overnight long-distance passenger run. This train has no fewer than seven material-handling cars at its head end as it passes Mexico, Pa., on the former Pennsylvania Railroad Middle Division. *Brian Solomon*

A forklift unloads RoadRailers at the back of train No. 89, the *Palmetto,* at Staples Mills Road station in Richmond, Va., on February 16, 2004. For a few years starting in the late 1990s, RoadRailer trailers were a routine sight on many Amtrak long-distance trains. *Brian Solomon*

Viewliner II baggage car 61044 brings up the rear of the consist on train No. 19, the New York-New Orleans *Crescent,* at Washington Union Station in 2018. It's one of 65 Viewliner II baggage cars, a type that began regular operations on long-distance trains in 2015.
Brian Solomon

weight streamliners seemed to offer a means of lowering operating costs.

Although these applications proved commercial failures, Talgo continued to successfully advance its train designs, eventually developing markets in Spain and elsewhere in Europe. In 1988, Amtrak imported a Spanish-built Talgo Prototipo de Alta Velocidad set to conduct high-speed tests on the Northeast Corridor. Then in 1994, the Washington State Department of Transportation (WSDOT) leased a 12-car TP-200 imported from Spain. This briefly operated in tests on the Northeast Corridor in March before entering a 6 month demonstration service in the Pacific Northwest in April. This sophisticated train employed an advanced pendular suspension that further reduced the effects of centrifugal forces on passengers, resulting in a very comfortable ride though curves at higher speeds. Success with this pendular Talgo led to more extensive applications of Talgo services in Washington and Oregon branded as Amtrak *Cascades.*

In 1996, to expand service on the north-south Eugene, Ore.-Seattle-Vancouver, B.C. route, WSDOT signed a unique lease-purchase deal with Talgo for two new Series VI trainsets. Amtrak

also exercised an option to purchase two more trainsets. The deal included a short-term lease of another TP200 trainset while the Series VI sets were under construction.

Series VI car bodies were built in Rivabellosa, Spain and assembled in Seattle in 1998. These new trains featured an innovative exterior design and Northwest-themed color scheme created by Amtrak Chief Designer César Vergara for the Amtrak *Cascades* brand. Vergara aimed to make these trains distinctive, attractive, and exciting to ride. Vergara also introduced a significant design innovation in the large formed

Top: Amtrak theatre/inspection car 10004, *American View,* had only been in service a few weeks when it passed through Mount Tom, Mass., on December 30, 2014. It's on the rear of train No. 55 (the southbound *Vermonter*) just a couple of days after the train assumed operations over the former Boston & Maine line between Springfield and East Northfield, Mass. This improvement shortened the *Vermonter's* running time, as the train from its 1995 inception had traversed a dogleg route over New England Central and CSX that required a reverse move at Palmer, Mass. *Brian Solomon*

Bottom: A San Jose-bound *Capitol* rolls along San Pablo Bay at Pinole, Calif., on May 3, 2008. The train has a typical consist of bilevel California cars led by an F59PHI styled and painted to match the train. The original California cars were built in the mid-1990s for Caltrans by Amerail, while 6462 *Moss Beach* (behind the F59) is a California Surfliner car built in 2003 by Alstom. *Brian Solomon*

fiberglass fins that provided a pleasing visual transition between the tall, streamlined F59PHI diesels and the low-profile cars.

Talgo also built a fifth Series VI set for an anticipated Los Angeles-Las Vegas service that never came to be. This was identical to the Amtrak *Cascades*, except it was dressed in a blue, black, and silver livery similar to the Pacific *Surfliner*. Following demonstrations and display in Arizona and California, it was added to the Seattle-based fleet and later purchased by WSDOT.

In total, 66 individual Talgo cars were built in a variety of configurations

The last car in this *Pacific Surfliner* push-pull consist is cab-control coach/baggage 6952. It's on San Diego-bound train No. 774, rolling along the beach at San Clemente, Calif., on November 16, 2018. The sleek double-deck Surfliner cars were built by Alstom at Hornell, N.Y., beginning in 2000. *Brian Solomon*

A power car brings up the rear of a new Talgo Series VI train at Railfair '99 at Sacramento, Calif. This view shows the large fiberglass fins on the roof, which were designed by César Vergara to make for a visually pleasing transition between the low-profile Talgo cars and standard-height F59PHI diesel locomotives. This set was built for a proposed Los Angeles-Las Vegas service that failed to materialize, so instead it was later assigned to Amtrak Cascades service in the Pacific Northwest. *Tom Kline*

A San Diego-bound *Pacific Surfliner* pauses at Santa Ana, Calif., on August 4, 2016. Amtrak California No. 6806 is one of eight similar bilevel Pacific business class Surfliner cars built by Alstom at Hornell, N.Y., in 2000. Note the difference in the stainless steel side and roof fluting between the Superliner (left) and Surfliner cars. *Brian Solomon*

for the five trainsets plus necessary spares. Each car measures approximately 46 feet long — significantly shorter than conventional passenger cars. The fleet includes two varieties of end cars with fins, six head-end power cars (which supply Amtrak-standard HEP independent of the locomotive), six baggage cars, 26 standard coaches, five business-class cars, 11 food-service cars (bistros and dining cars), plus seven coaches and five business-class cars configured to comply with Americans with Disabilities Act (ADA) accessibility requirements including wheelchair lifts.

The Series VI trains were designed to meet international safety standards, which were slightly different than those mandated in the United States. In order operate in regular service, the carbodies required an FRA waiver for non-compliance with the 800,000-pound buff compression standard.

The Series VI trains served as the core of Amtrak Cascades services for more than 20 years. They won industrial design awards from the Art Institute of Chicago in 1998 and the Smithsonian Institution in 2003. The trains were named for mountains in the Pacific Northwest: *Mount Adams, Mount*

Baker, Mount Hood, Mount Olympia, and *Mount Rainier.*

Despite being popular with riders and prized for their design, in June 2020 the trains were prematurely withdrawn from service. This was partly as a fallout from the disastrous fatal accident on December 17, 2017, when the inaugural run over the new Point Defiance Bypass derailed as result of an overspeed incident, and from a temporary drop in ridership during the COVID-19 pandemic. WSDOT sold its trainsets for scrap in 2022; Amtrak's sets were scrapped 2 years later. One Talgo Series VI Bistro car, 7304, has been preserved at the Northwest Railway Museum in Snoqualmie, Wash.

In 2009, Wisconsin DOT looked to Talgo to supply trains for an anticipated expansion of the Chicago-Milwaukee *Hiawatha* Service to Madison, Wis. The company adapted its pendular design to fully comply with FRA crashworthiness, with resistance to telescoping, rollover, and accordion-damage scenarios. Wisconsin ordered a pair of Series 8 trains built for a 125-mph top speed. This was an effort by Talgo to establish a stronger presence in the American market and to

This trailing view shows Talgo Series VI set *Mount Hood* working as Amtrak *Cascades* train No. 501 (Seattle-Portland). It's passing Pioneer interlocking at Chambers Bay Beach, Wash. Each of the five Series VI trains were named for iconic Pacific Northwest mountain peaks. *Jeffrey T. Schultz*

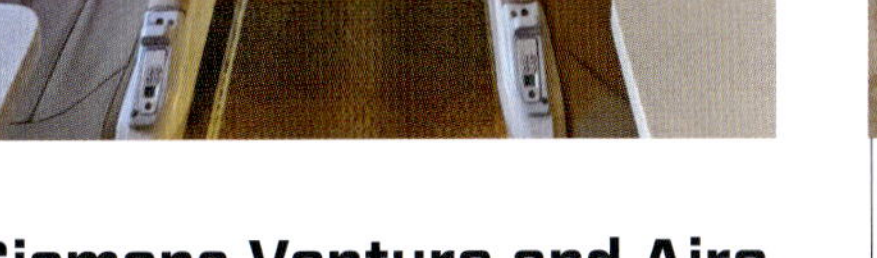

comply with Buy America requirements. In doing so, the company set up a factory in Milwaukee. Unfortunately, these trains got caught in political rift that ultimately resulted in Wisconsin canceling the order before the new trains turned a wheel in *Hiawatha* service.

About the same time, Oregon DOT worked with Talgo for a pair of 13-Car Series 8 Talgo trains similar to those under construction for Wisconsin, also built in Milwaukee. Delivered in 2013, these were named *Mount Bachelor* and *Mount Jefferson* and assigned to Amtrak Cascades service. They feature a variety of car configurations similar to those on Series VI trains which allow the trains to be fully accessible. Among the distinctive features of the these trains is the purpose-built push-pull control cab at one end of the train that features a leading-end B-style truck.

Washington DOT was offered an option to purchase the orphaned Wisconsin trainsets, but declined. Subsequently the Wisconsin sets were sold and exported to Nigeria.

Siemens Venture and Airo

In recent years Amtrak has begun replacement of its older passenger equipment. State-sponsored services in California and the Midwest have ordered Siemens Mobility's Venture push-pull trainsets. These single-level trains offer passengers a variety of state-of-the-art amenities in an ergonomical environment with maximum ADA accessibility. Cars are equipped with modern fabricated trucks and air-spring suspension, with roof-mounted HVAC for climate control. Weatherproof gangway connections are intended as an improvement over traditional vestibules. Interior accommodation includes reclining seats with large picture windows featuring integrated window roller shades.

Several types of cars make up the new trainsets. Intermediate economy cars feature up to 74 seats per car (62 seats in the cab-control car. Business class offers greater space for individual passengers with a maximum of 54 seats. Café cars have seating for up to 44.

Amtrak California services began trial runs with Siemens Venture equip-

Above, left to right: The elegant, distinctively styled Talgo Series VI *Cascades* trainsets were an exceptional achievement in modern American intercity passenger service and the source of great pride for the men and women involved with trains. The Bistro, left, was always the best feature of the Series VI; passengers and employees loved it because it was a beautiful modern railcar. Bistro 7304 has been preserved by the Northwest Railway Museum. The Series VI coaches, middle, offered distinctive styling and comfortable seating that was very popular with passengers. An onboard plaque, right, salutes those involved in getting the trainsets into service. *Three photos: Jeffrey T. Schultz*

Top: On April 18, 2023, a *Hiawatha* train consisting of new Siemens Mobility Venture cars pauses at Sturtevant, Wis. The modern station was opened in 2006, replacing the former Milwaukee Road depot in downtown Sturtevant approximately a mile south. *Chris Guss*

Bottom: In a vision of contemporary Amtrak state-supported operations, Illinois Department of Transportation SC44 diesels are positioned at both ends of a train of brand-new Venture Cars on a Milwaukee-Chicago *Hiawatha* near A2 Tower in Chicago. The diesels and cars are all products of Siemens' Mobility Division plant in Sacramento, Calif. *Patrick Yough*

ment in late 2023, and trains with the equipment were officially launched on Oakland-Bakersfield-San Joaquin trains in March 2024. Similar Venture cars for Chicago-based Midwestern services entered service a few months later.

In late 2022, Amtrak announced an order for Siemens Airo intercity trainsets as replacements for Amfleet I cars, many of which were approaching 5 decades of service. In 2023, Amtrak increased its order to a total of 83 Airo trainsets, each of which has six to eight cars semipermanently coupled together. The first are expected to make a public debut in 2026.

Similar to the Venture equipment, the push-pull Airo trains are being manufactured by Siemens at its Sacramento, Calif., plant. They're expected to share styling with Amtrak's long-distance Charger locomotives (ALC42). Dan Cupper reported on Trains.com in December 2022 that the design is pattered after Siemens' Viaggio Comfort fleet of electric-propelled trains operated in European intercity service by ÖBB (Austrian Federal Railway). The trains are designed to work with a power car, which in many cases is expected to be a new dual-mode type to allow for service on electrified and non-electrified lines without the need to change

locomotives. Maximum service speed will be 125 mph.

Amtrak promotional materials tout that the new passenger cars will have spacious, comfortable seating, with modern Wi-Fi connections and other amenities. Business-class cars will feature two-by-one seating to give passengers a choice of arrangements.

Airo sets are expected to serve a variety of medium- and long-distance trains and routes in the East, including Northeast Regional, Empire Service, *Downeaster, Adirondack, Vermonter, Maple Leaf, Ethan Allen Express, Carolinian, Palmetto, Pennsylvanian,* and *Keystone,* as well as on Amtrak Cascades service in the Pacific Northwest — where the trains are expected to make their service debut.

Among the distinctive features of the Talgo Series 8 trains is the cab-control car, as this one leading the *Mount Bachelor* trainset. Two Series 8 trains were purchased for Amtrak *Cascades* service.
Jeffrey T. Schultz

BIBLIOGRAPHY

Books

The Designs of Raymond Loewy. Washington D.C. 1975.

National Transportation Policy Study Commission. *National Transportation Policies Through the year 2000.* Washington D.C., 1979.

All Stations: A Journey Through 150 years of Railway History. Paris, 1978

Allen, G. Freeman. *The Fastest Trains in the World.* London, 1978.

Anderson, Craig T. *Amtrak — The National Rail Passenger Corporation 1978-1979 Annual.* San Francisco, Calif., 1978

Armstrong, John H. *The Railroad — What it is, What it Does.* Omaha, Neb., 1982.

Bradley, Rodger. *Amtrak — The U.S. National Railroad Passenger Corporation.* Poole, Dorset, U.K., 1985.

Bush, Donald J. *The Streamlined Decade.* New York, 1975.

Churella, Albert, J. *From Steam to Diesel.* Princeton, N.J., 1998

Condit, Carl, *Port of New York,* Vols. 1 and 2. Chicago, 1980, 1981.

Cupper, Dan. *Horseshoe Heritage, The Story of a Great Railroad Landmark.* Halifax, Pa. 1996.

Daughen, Joseph R., and Peter Binzen. *The Wreck of the Penn Central.* Boston, 1971.

Del Grosso, Robert C. *Burlington Northern 1980-1991 Annual.* Denver, Colo., 1991

Diehl, Lorraine B. *The Late Great Pennsylvania Station.* New York, 1985.

Diesel Era. *The Revolutionary Diesel — EMC's FT.* Halifax, Pa., 1994.

Doherty, Timothy Scott, and Brian Solomon. *Conrail.* St. Paul, Minn., 2004.

Dorin, Patrick. *Amtrak — Trains & Travel.* Seattle, Wash., 1979.

Droege, John A. *Passenger Terminals and Trains.* New York, 1916.

Drury, George H. *The Historical Guide to North American Railroads.* Waukesha, Wis., 1985.

Duke, Donald, and Edmund Keilty. *RDC: The Budd Rail Diesel Car.* San Marino, Calif., 1990.

Farrington, Jr., S. Kip. *Railroads at War.* New York, 1944.

——. *Railroading from the Rear End.* New York, 1946.

——. *Railroads of Today.* New York, 1949

Fischler, Stan. *Next Stop Grand Central.* Ontario, 1986.

Frailey, Fred W. *Zephyrs, Chiefs & Other Orphans — The First Five Years of Amtrak.* Godfrey, Ill, 1977.

Garmany, John B. *Southern Pacific Dieselization.* Edmonds, Wash., 1985.

Harlow, Alvin F. *Steelways of New England.* New York, 1946.

————. *The Road of the Century.* New York, 1947.

Hofsommer, Don. L. *Southern Pacific 1900-1985.* College Station, Texas, 1986.

Hollingsworth, Brian. *Modern Trains.* London, 1985.

Hollingsworth, Brian and Arthur Cook. *Modern Locomotives.* London, 1983.

Jones, Robert W. *Boston & Albany: The New York Central in New England,* Vols. 1 & 2. Los Angeles, 1997.

————. *Boston & Maine — Forest, River and Mountain.* Los Angeles, 2000.

Keilty, Edmund. *Interurbans Without Wires.* Glendale, Calif., 1979.

Kirkland, John, F. *Dawn of the Diesel Age.* Pasadena, Calif., 1994.

Kirkland, John, F. *The Diesel Builders* Vols. I, II, and III. Glendale, Calif., 1983

Klein, Maury. *Union Pacific,* Vols. I & II. New York, 1989.

Loewy, Raymond. *The Locomotive* (Its Esthetics). New York, 1937.

Lyon, Peter. *To Hell in a Day Coach.* Philadelphia, 1968.

Marre, Louis A. and Jerry A. Pinkepank. *The Contemporary Diesel Spotter's Guide.* Milwaukee, Wis., 1985.

————. *Diesel Locomotives: The First 50 Years.* Waukesha, Wis., 1995.

Marre, Louis A. and Paul K. Withers. *The Contemporary Diesel Spotter's Guide,* Year 2000 Edition. Halifax, Pennsylvania, 2000.

Middleton, William D. *When the Steam Railroads Electrified.* Milwaukee, 1974.

————. *Manhattan Gateway: New York's Pennsylvania Station.* Waukesha, Wisconsin, 1996.

————. *From Bullets to BART.* Chicago, 1989.

Mulhearn, Daniel J. and John R. Taibi. *General Motors' F-Units.* New York, 1982.

Pinkepank, Jerry A. *The Diesel Spotter's Guide.* Milwaukee, Wis., 1967.

————. *The Second Diesel Spotter's Guide.* Milwaukee, Wis., 1973.

Potter, Janet Greenstein. *Great American Railroad Stations.* New York, 1996.

Reck, Franklin M. *On Time. Electro-Motive Division of General Motors,* 1948.

————. *The Dilworth Story.* New York, 1954.

Riddell, Doug. *From the Cab.* Pasadena, Calif., 1999.

Ryan, Dennis and Joseph Shine. *Southern Pacific Passenger Trains.* Vols. 1 & 2. La Mirada, Calif., 1986, 2000.

Saunders, Richard, Jr. *The Railroad Mergers and the Coming of Conrail.* Westport, Conn. 1978.

————.*Merging Lines: American Railroads 1900-1970.* DeKalb, Ill., 2001

Schafer, Mike. *All Aboard Amtrak.* Piscataway, NJ, 1991.

Snopek, Joseph R., and Robert A. La May. *Diesels to Park Avenue.* Granby, Mass., 1997.

Solomon, Brian. *The American Diesel Locomotive.* Osceola, Wis., 1999.

————. *Railroad Stations.* New York, 1998

————. *GE Locomotives.* St. Paul, Minn., 2003.

————. *Amtrak.* St. Paul, Minn., 2004.

————. *EMD F-unit Locomotives.* North Branch, Minn., 2005.

————. *Southern Pacific Passenger Trains.* St. Paul, MN, 2005.

————. *EMD Locomotives.* St. Paul, Minn., 2006.

————. *Railroads of Pennsylvania.* Minneapolis, Minn., 2008.

————. *Alco Locomotives.* Minneapolis, Minn., 2009.

————. *Electro-Motive E-Units and F-Units.* St. Paul, Mn., 2011.

————. *Field Guide to Trains: Locomotives and Rolling Stock,* St. Paul, Minn., 2016.

Solomon, Brian and Timothy Scott Doherty. *Conrail.* Osceola, Wis., 2004.

Staufer, Alvin F., and Edward L. May. *New York Central's Later Power 1910-1968.* Medina, Ohio

Staufer, Alvin F. *Pennsy Power II.* Medina, Ohio, 1968.

Steinbrenner, Richard T. *The American Locomotive Company—A Centennial Remembrance.* Warren, New Jersey, 2003.

Thompson, Slason. *Short History of American Railways.* Chicago, 1925.

Thoms, William E. *Reprieve for the Iron Horse — the Amtrak Experiment — its Predecessors and Prospects.* Baton Rouge, La, 1973.

Trewman, H.F. *Electrification of Railways.* London, 1920.

Warner, David C., and Bruce Goldberg. *The Metroliners — Trains that Changed the Course of American Rail Travel.* Bucklin, Mo., 2016.

Westing, Frederic. *Penn Station: Its Tunnels and Side Rodders.* Seattle, 1977.

Wilner, Frank N. *The Amtrak Story.* Omaha, Neb., 1994.

White, John H. Jr. *A History of the American Locomotive — Its Development: 1830-1880.* Baltimore, Johns Hopkins Press, 1968.

————. *The American Railroad Passenger Car,* Vols. I & II. Baltimore, Johns Hopkins Press, 1978.

Wright, Richard K. *Southern Pacific Day-*

light. Thousand Oaks, Calif., 1970.
Zimmermann, Karl R. *The Remarkable GG1.* New York, 1977.
———. *Amtrak at Milepost 10.* Park Forest, Ill., 1981.

Periodicals

Classic Trains, Waukesha, Wis.
CTC Board — Railroads Illustrated, Ferndale, Wash.
Diesel Era, Halifax, Pa.
Diesel Railway Traction, supplement to *Railway Gazette* (UK). (merged into *Railway Gazette*).
Extra 2200 South, Cincinnati, Ohio. [no longer published].
Jane's World Railways. London.
Locomotive & Railway Preservation. Waukesha, Wis. [no longer published].
Official Guide to the Railways. New York.
Passenger Train Journal, Waukesha, Wis., and Bucklin, Mo.
Passenger Train Annual, Nos. 3 & 4, Park Forest, Ill. [no longer published].
RailNews. Waukesha, Wis. [no longer published].
Railroad History, formerly *Railway and Locomotive Historical Society Bulletin.* Boston, Mass., and Harrisburg, Pa.
Railway Age, Chicago and New York.
Railway Mechanical Engineer.
Railway Signaling and Communications, formerly *The Railway Signal Engineer,* nèe *Railway Signaling.* Chicago and New York.
The Railway Gazette, London.
Trains. Waukesha, Wis.
Today's Railways. Sheffield, United Kingdom.
Vintage Rails. Waukesha, Wis. [no longer published]

Railroad company literature and publications

Amtrak Passenger Trains, 1990.
Amtrak public timetables 1971 to 2016.
Chicago, Burlington & Quincy. *Burlington's big new Vista-Dome Denver Zephyr.*
Chicago, Milwaukee, St. Paul & Pacific public timetables 1943-1966.
Chicago & North Western System public timetables 1945-1960.
Conrail, Pittsburgh Division, System Timetable No. 5, 1997.
Electro-Motive Division SDP40F Operator's Manual, 2nd Edition. LaGrange, Illinois, 1974.
General Electric. Dash 8 Locomotive Line. (no date)
General Electric P32AC-DM Operating Manual. Erie, Pa., 1995.
General Motors. Electro-Motive Division Operating Manual No. 2300. La Grange, Ill., c1945.
General Motors. Electro-Motive Division Model F3 Operating Manual No. 2308B. La Grange, Ill., 1948.
General Motors. Electro-Motive Division Model 567B Engine Maintenance Manual. La Grange, Ill., 1948
General Motors. Electro-Motive Division, Diesel Locomotive Operating Manual No. 2312 for Model GP7 with Vapor Car Steam Generator. 2nd Edition. La Grange, Ill., 1950.
General Motors. Electro-Motive Division Model F7 Operating Manual No. 2310. La Grange, Ill., 1951.
General Motors. Electro-Motive Division Model F9 Operating Manual No. 2315. La Grange, Ill., 1954.
General Motors. Electro-Motive Division, Diesel Locomotive Operating Manual No. 2318 for Model GP9. 3rd Edition. La Grange, Ill., 1957.
Metro-North Commuter Railroad. Operator's Manual FL9-AC Locomotive. 1993.
Metro-North Railroad, Rules of the Operating Department, 1999.
Metro-North Railroad, Timetable No. 1. 2001.
NRE Locomotive, N-ViroMotive 2GS12B Tier IV Switcher Specification General Data. (no date).
NORAC Operating Rules, 7th Edition. 2000.
Pennsylvania Railroad public timetables 1942-1968.
Pennsylvania Railroad. Modern Power for Today's Trains. No date.
Santa Fe public timetables 1943-1969.
Siemens Mobility, *America's Passenger Rail Experience Charger I Diesel-Electric Passenger Locomotive.* New York, 2020.
Southern Pacific Company. Public timetables 1930-1958.
Southern Pacific Lines. Western Region Timetable 3. 1989.
TurboTrain Rail Speed, Convenience, Comfort. United Aircraft Corporate System Center. c1967.

Papers and original manuscripts

Kettering, Eugene W. *History and Development of the 567 Series General Motors Locomotive Engine.* Atlantic City, New Jersey, 1951.
Louis T. Klauder and Associates Consulting Engineers. *The Pennsylvania Railroad Specifications for Electric Multiple Unit Railroad Passenger Cars.* c1965.
USDOT FRA High Cant Deficiency Test of the LRC train, the AEM-7 locomotive and the Amcoach. Report no. DOT-FR-81-06. Patrick L. Boyd, Robert E. Scofield, Joseph P. Zaiko, 1982.
USDOT FRA Safety Relevant Observations on the X2000 Train as Developed for the Swedish National Railways. DOT/FRA/ORD-90/14, 1990.
USDOT FRA Vehicle Performance Test: Material Handling Cars in Service from New York City to Chicago. 2003.
USEPA Office of Mobile Sources. Regulatory Announcement. Final Emissions Standards for Locomotives. 1997.

Amtrak Company Documents
Amtrak-acs64-cities-sprinter
Amtrak-ACS-64-locomotives-case-study
Amtrak-Airo-Built-by-America-10.12.2023c
Amtrak Operating Instructions F40PH/P30CH diesel-electric locomotives, 1983.
California Car Operating Manual. Amtrak California, 1997.
F40 Locomotive Reliability Study, Mechanical Department Western Region, 1994.
High-Speed Trainset, Operating Instruction Manual.
Specification for PRIIA Bi-Level Passenger Car; PRIIA Specification No. 305-001,
Amtrak Specification No. 962. 2012

Internet sources

amtrak.com
asm.transitdoc.com
assets.new.siemens.com
cummins.com
nepis.epa.gov
on-track-on-line.com
railjournal.com
railroads.dot.gov/sites/fra.dot.gov
railwaygazette.com
siemens.com
timetables.org/browse/
trainweb.org
usa.siemens.com/mobility
wsdot.wa.gov